CONFUCIANISM
ITS RELEVANCE TO MODERN SOCIETY

MARTIN LU

FEDERAL PUBLICATIONS
Singapore · Kuala Lumpur · Hong Kong

© 1983 Federal Publications (S) Pte Ltd
Times Jurong
2 Jurong Port Road
Singapore 2261

Printed by Kyodo-Shing Loong Printing Industries Pte Ltd

ISBN 9971 4 3147 5

Preface

As the title indicates, this book aims at clarifying to the layman what Confucianism is, and why it is relevant to Singapore today. With the recent announcement by the Ministry of Education of its intention to incorporate Confucian ethics into the curriculum of moral education for Secondary 3 and 4 students, Confucianism will, from now on, play a vital and prominent role in our educational system.

If Confucius were alive today, he would be surprised and delighted to witness the renaissance of his teachings in Singapore. Despite the long-standing presence of Chinese culture, English education and Western influence have increasingly gained ground here in recent years. So how do we explain the sudden limelight shone upon the ethics of this Chinese sage? We can understand why Confucian values have been enthusiastically embraced by some of the Chinese-educated Singaporeans. But why should they receive the official blessings of a government which in many respects is pragmatic, modern and thoroughly Western?

Many English-educated Singaporeans are particularly puzzled about this Confucian renaissance. For all their respect and even admiration for the Chinese sage, they cannot help viewing the matter with certain mixed feelings. Confucianism, of course, is part of Chinese culture, and as such should be cherished. Indeed, there is an increasing tendency for people to search for and identify themselves with their cultural roots. But to have emotional nostalgia for our cultural heritage is one thing; to seriously consider making it a guide to our modern living is entirely another. They would regard this current revival of Confucian ethics as an impractical and backward move in the evolution of culture.

The above reservation is not completely unfounded. Is there not an enormous gulf between the society of Confucius' time and ours today? It would be foolish to pretend that all his ideas are relevant now. But I shall try to show that many of them are: for instance, the stress upon familial and social harmony and cohesion, the importance of moral character, and the optimism about man's inherent ability for the moral good. Although we have made tremendous progress in many fields during our time, unfortunately the general quality of our human relations does not seem to benefit much from all our efforts towards modernization. It is therefore vital in our present study of Confucianism to distinguish its relevant features from the not so relevant aspects. And even among the relevant values it is the perspective and not the details that really matters.

Before we can answer such questions about the Confucian renaissance as mentioned above, we should first understand what Confucianism is. Furthermore, to acquire some knowledge of Confucianism is a rewarding experience in itself: for the Chinese, to establish some rapport with their cultural roots; and for the non-Chinese, to become acquainted with a great tradition.

Consequently, this book is structured as follows. In Part One, I provide a simple account of Confucianism. I begin with a general outline, a kind of bird's-eye view, and then examine some central concepts, such as human nature, immortality, and the harmony between 'Heaven and man'. Then in Part Two, I examine the relevance of Confucianism to Singapore today.

It goes without saying that this book is far from definitive on many points. A succinct exposition of Confucianism is difficult enough, and the problem of the relationship between Confucian and modern values in a society such as ours is even more so. I can only hope that this work will contribute in a small way to the understanding and debate of the problems concerned. I also hope that it expresses my own views clearly and distinctly enough to facilitate the fulfilment of this task.

June 1982

Martin Lu Ph. D.
Department of Philosophy
National University of Singapore

Contents

Contents

1

What is Confucianism?
(A Bird's-Eye View)

'Confucianism' is the English term for *Ru Jia* (儒家), which literally means the School of Scholars. To throw some light on Confucianism, it is useful to know the background and social function of those people who, during Confucius' time, were considered as the *Ru* (儒), the Confucianists.

There are two theories regarding this. According to the first, the *Ru* people were the descendants of the Shang people, whose dynasty was overthrown by the Chou people in the twelfth century B.C. Because they were a conquered people, they preached the virtue of weakness to protect themselves. As they were now disinherited and dispossessed, they had to find a new way of making a living through their knowledge of classic learning, music, and rituals. They thus became assistants in sacrifices, funerals, marriages and other ceremonial functions.

The second theory maintains that, far from being the descendants of the Shang tribe, these *Ru* people were members of the Chou royal family disinherited as a result of the disintegration and downfall of the feudal system. Having forfeited their official ranks and remuneration, they found it easier to make a living through their knowledge of ancient classics and rituals.

This knowledge consists mainly of the six arts[1], which include ceremonials and music, history (or writing) and numbers, archery and charioteering. These were the subjects of their previous noble education, which proved useful to the feudal princes at that time. Consequently these *Ru* people found a new career to compensate for their loss of privileged positions and revenues. Besides, they were also potential office-seekers. These social positions and functions of Confucianists have generally remained unchanged throughout Chinese history.

The above depiction may also explain why Confucianism has often been considered conservative and orthodox. Being transmitters of classic learning. Confucianists feel it their mission to carry on the cultural heritage. Even though they may inject new ideas into classic learning in the process of transmission, they have the penchant for glorifying and expressing their indebtedness to what is old. Occasionally when a great Confucianist emerged, a new direction or a fresh perspective was taken to develop or interpret the original Confucian ideas. The drawback of this mentality is the relative lack of diversity and originality in Chinese thought compared with their Western counterparts. Nevertheless, the Chinese mind is thereby provided with a more stable and continuous orientation.

There has been a tendency among laymen to identify Confucianism only with Confucius' philosophy. This misconception hampers a deeper understanding of the richness and complexity within Confucianism. Although Confucius was the founder and thus the most prominent member of this school, his ideas are very much different from those of Mencius, Xun Zi (荀子), as well as of the later Confucianists. All these different ideas must be included as part of Confucianism. In its broad sense, Confucianism comprises the ideas and doctrines of all the Confucianists in the history of Chinese philosophy. Hence, to study Confucianism more thoroughly and comprehensively, we should trace the evolution of its various transformations throughout Chinese history. Any attempt to identify Confucianism merely with Confucius' philosophy tends to over-simplify the matter.

What is a Confucianist? Subjectively he must be willing to identify his ideology with Confucianism; objectively he must at least share the basic tenets and doctrines of Confucianism even if some of his interpretations prove to be original. Historically, apart from Confucius, the prominent Confucianists include Mencius and Xun Zi during the Pre-Qin period (Qin 秦 refers to the dynasty which lasted from 221-206 B.C.). During the Han dynasty (汉 206 B.C. -220 A.D.) there were Dong Zhong-Shu(董仲舒) and Yang Xiong (杨雄). Then in the Tang dynasty (唐 618-907 A.D.) Han Yu (韩愈) and Li Ao (李翱) attempted to revive Confucianism after a long period of domination by Taoism and Buddhism.

Their efforts ushered in the era of Song(宋 960-1279 A.D.) and Ming (明 1368-1644 A.D.) Neo-Confucianists, the first golden period of Confucianism since the Pre-Qin age. The major thinkers during this period included Zhou Dun-yi (周敦颐), Shao Yong (邵雍), Zhang Zai (张载), Cheng Hao (程颢), and Cheng Yi (程颐), the so-called Five Masters of the Song dynasty. Their doctrines were later synthesized in the philosophy of Zhu Xi (朱熹), the chief representative of the 'School of Principle' (理学) within Neo-Confucianism. The two representatives of the Neo-Confucian 'School of Mind' (心学) were Lu Xiang-shan (陆象山) of the Song dynasty and Wang Yang-ming (王阳明) of the Ming dynasty.

The major point of contention between the two schools is this. According to the School of Principle, we have to investigate and understand the principle (the law of being) of each and every thing, and finally we shall be able to achieve enlightenment and an understanding of the principle. The School of Mind on the other hand holds that, since the principle is no other than the mind, to directly reflect upon the mind is the simpler and more straightforward way of grasping the principle. In fact, the difference is only one of approach: the underlying doctrines are fundamentally the same.

Because of the influence and challenge from Taoism and Buddhism, Song and Ming Neo-Confucianism can be characterized as metaphysical and speculative. This abstract and speculative learning is called the Song Learning. In the Qing dynasty, there was a movement to revolt against this speculative tendency. This movement followed the Han dynasty's tradition of 'Investigation Based on Evidence' (考证) and was labelled as the Han Learning. Nevertheless, the major thinkers of this period like Wang Fu-Zhi (王夫之), Yan Yuan (颜元), and Dai Zhen (戴震) generally retained their Confucian orientations albeit with a more naturalistic or practical bias. During the contemporary period, Feng You-lan (冯友兰, also transliterated as Fung Yu-lan) and Xiong Shi-li (熊十力) were the two major Confucianists representing the New Rationalistic Confucianism and the New Idealistic Confucianism respectively. (The latter is deceased and the former has recanted his previous philosophical position after 1949.)

In the light of the above historical delineation, it should therefore be clear that Confucianism is more than just Confucius' own philosophy and that to study Confucianism is to find one's way through its whole history. However, the essence of Confucianism lies in the philosophies of Confucius, Mencius and Xun

Zi which are mainly contained in the *Confucian Analects,* the *Book of Mencius,* the *Great Learning,* the *Doctrine of the Mean* (these four works are known as the *Four Books* compiled by Zhu Xi of the Song dynasty), and the *Xun Zi.* Some scholars may even want to include the supplementary chapters to the *Book of Changes* (*Yi Jing* 易经), known as the *Ten Wings* (十翼), as the source of Confucius' doctrines. But recent scholarship would treat only the *Analects* as the most reliable source. Since the discussion here is meant to present a bird's-eye view of Confucianism, we shall follow the traditional view without engaging into this highly complicated debate.

In other words, our view here is that Confucianism in its narrow sense covers only the Pre-Qin Confucianism, whereas in its broad sense Confucianism also comprises the Song and Ming Neo-Confucianism among others. The Pre-Qin Confucianism (also called Primordial Confucianism) and the Song and Ming Neo-Confucianism are generally considered the most philosophically rich periods of Confucianism. Nowadays, most university philosophy departments generally divide Confucianism and Neo-Confucianism into two separate courses. In a preliminary discussion here, we would regard the main tenets and doctrines of Pre-Qin Confucianism as constituting the essential features of Confucianism.

This is more the case, if we realize that these tenets and doctrines serve as the nuclear ideas for the development of later Confucian theories. We can therefore say that to understand Pre-Qin Confucianism is tantamount to understanding the essence of Confucianism. To bring some perspective to the understanding of Pre-Qin Confucianism, we must trace back to the prevailing cultural beliefs and conditions of the Shang dynasty (商 1751-1112 B.C.), which immediately preceded the Zhou (周 1111-249 B.C.). The Shang people believed that the transformations of natural phenomena have a direct link with human affairs. (For a more detailed account of this, refer to Chapter 4.)

This belief was further developed into the thinking that auspicious and inauspicious consequences could be predicted by experts on the basis of these natural phenomena. Whenever the aristocrats were about to engage in important events such as expeditions, hunting, or marriage, they would invariably consult the diviners. The unearthed oracle bones of the Shang dynasty are full

4

of divination records. It is therefore clear that the Shang people were extremely superstitious. Their submission to spiritual beings was almost total. After the Zhou people overthrew the Shang dynasty in 1111 B.C., they developed the famous doctrine of the 'Mandate of Heaven' (天命) to justify their right to rule. According to this doctrine, human destiny depends upon man's own moral efforts, and not upon spiritual forces. This is an extremely important doctrine in Confucianism, which inaugurated the new growth of humanism in Chinese history.

Up until then, supernatural power had dominated over human affairs. Now, for the first time, man's virtue could shape his own destiny, and, as a result, the future prospects of a dynasty depended upon the virtue of the ruler rather than any spiritual power. If the ruler possessed the virtue, he had the mandate to rule. If not, he would lose it. From then on, morality was not just this-worldly concern, but had some semi-religious or metaphysical implications. Furthermore, there was some metaphysical link between man's moral efforts and the will of Heaven, which is what is known as the oneness between Heaven and man (天人合一). For instance, it is stated in the *Doctrine of the Mean:* 'It is characteristic of absolute sincerity to be able to foreknow. When a nation or family is about to flourish, there are sure to be lucky omens. When a nation or family is about to perish, there are sure to be unlucky omens.'[2]

Traces of Pre-Confucian superstitions still linger. Yet, owing to the humanistic influences of Confucius, the will of Heaven did not now operate arbitrarily. Philosophically, this concept is the key to understanding many Confucian doctrines. Heaven as an anthropomorphic being in the Shang dynasty was now transformed in the Zhou dynasty into Heaven as the moral or metaphysical entity. The Mandate of Heaven as introduced by the Zhou people had two important philosophical implications. First, man's moral efforts became more important, which inaugurated a new era of humanism. Second, man's link to Heaven provided a metaphysical ground for his moral efforts and thus gave them a more profound significance far transcending this corporeal life. The philosophical importance of Confucius lies in his furtherance of these two implications, developing them to a higher plane.

In studying Confucius' humanism, the most crucial concept is *ren* (仁), which has been variously translated in English as love, benevolence, human-heartedness, perfect virtue, or humanity. The word *ren* does not appear too often in Pre-Confucian texts. When it does appear, it denotes the particular virtue of kindness in a ruler towards his subjects. It was Confucius who transformed it into a virtue achievable by everyone, broadened it to become a comprehensive virtue covering all individual Confucian virtues, and finally elevated it to become the centre of his philosophy. Although Confucius occasionally still treated *ren* as a particular virtue, *ren* in most cases represented for him the all-inclusive substance of morality. Yet in both senses *ren* has dropped its original meaning of aristocratic virtue. This must be taken as a democratization of an important philosophic concept.[3]

To further illustrate this concept, let us study the following statements:

1   Few of those who are filial sons and respectful brothers will show disrespect to superiors, and there has never been a man who is not disrespectful to superiors and yet creates disorder. ... Filial piety and brotherly respect are the root of *ren*.[4]

2   A man with clever words and an ingratiating appearance is seldom a man of *ren*.[5]

3   If a man is not *ren* (humane), what has he to do with ceremonies (*li* 礼)? If he is not *ren*, what has he to do with music?[6]

4   Only the man of *ren* knows how to love people and hate people.[7]

5   A man who is strong, resolute, simple, and slow to speak is near to *ren*.[8]

Here we see only the specific manifestations of *ren* as applied to different situations. It would be philosophically inconsistent to treat them as different definitions of *ren*. Confucius was primarily interested in showing how *ren*, the substance of morality, functions in various situations. He might have been of the opinion that if one was familiar with the various manifestations of *ren* in different concrete situations, a certain moral insight regarding this important moral substance could be achieved.[9]

We can also look at the problem from another perspective, which tends to delve deeply into the heart of Confucianism. According to this perspective, the basic concern in Confucianism is how to become a sage. To attain this goal, one must not only realize *ren* in one's nature but also extend it to society at large, which involves *li,* the rules of propriety. This view is persuasively expounded by the following argument:

> . . . it is misleading to argue that since sagehood is inherent in the nature of man, the attainment of sagehood requires nothing more than a process of inner transformation, independent of society at large. This being so, self-transformation must be regarded as both a means and an end in the process of self-extension. In fact it points to a dialectical interplay between the means of self-cultivation as internal examination and the end of complete self-realization as communion with others and with the universe at large.[10]

It is therefore clear that the self-realization of *ren* is not just a matter of self-transformation of selfhood in human nature but is also a matter of communion with others. In other words, the full realization of *ren* is inseparable from one's relationship with others, which is what Confucius emphasized in his depiction of the various manifestations of *ren. Ren* expresses this extension from the self to others in terms of *zhong* (忠) 'conscientiousness to others' and *shu* (恕) 'altruism'. *Zhong* means 'Desiring to establish oneself, one also establishes others; desiring to develop oneself, one also develops others.'[11] This is equivalent to what we generally regard as the Golden Rule, 'Do to others what you would like others to do to you.' *Shu* can be interpreted as 'Do not do to others what you do not wish others to do to you."[12] This can be considered the Silver Rule, as it addresses itself to the negative aspect of the Golden Rule.

From the philosophical point of view, we are not satisfied with treating *ren* on the basis of its manifestations only. We would like to go even further, to tackle the concept of *ren* per se. For a more systematic and detailed study of *ren,* we have to refer to Mencius through the theoretical linkage of the *Great Learning* and the *Doctrine of the Mean.* Without wrangling about the dating of these two works, we would like to accept the verdict of traditional scholarship that these two works were formulated after Confucius and before Mencius. According to this view, the *Great Learning* was developed and transmitted by Zeng Zi (曾子), Confucius' disciple; the *Doctrine of the Mean* was written by Zi Si (子思), Confucius' grandson, and handed down to Mencius. We further maintain that fundamentally there is no disparity between these two works, which simply developed and continued Confucius' tradition and passed it on to Mencius. This represents the orthodox line of Confucius' heritage.

Our approach here is to accept as the foundation of Confucian orthodoxy the three items (三纲领) of the *Great Learning* as interpreted from the perspective of the opening statement of the *Doctrine of the Mean*. According to the three items, Confucian moral cultivation is a matter of working from within and extending to external human relationships. For instance, the first item is 'manifesting the clear character of man' (明明德). In order to fully appreciate its meaning, we must refer to the opening statements in the *Doctrine of the Mean:* 'What man receives from Heaven is his nature; to act in accordance with his nature is the moral truth (Dao); to cultivate this moral truth is education.' Here we have one of the most important doctrines in Confucianism, i.e. human nature is what Heaven imparts to man. Furthermore, this human nature embodies moral standards originated from Heaven, the metaphysical source of the universe. And to cultivate and develop the moral truth within human nature is the Confucian concept of education. Hence the Confucian theory of education has its foundation in Confucian moral philosophy. The above statements from the *Doctrine of the Mean* constitute the foundation for both.

With this in mind, we should then understand the meaning of 'manifesting the clear character of man'. To manifest the clear character means to manifest the character as bestowed upon us by Heaven. The clear character is the moral character or the character as it ought to be if man simply acts in accordance with his Heaven-bestowed nature. The further extension of manifesting the clear character is 'loving the people' (亲民), the second item of the *Great Learning*. As love is fully extended, there is the complete realization of *ren,* which is tantamount to 'abiding in the highest good' (止于至善), the third item. Besides the three items, the *Great Learning* also consists of the eight steps (八条目), which are the ways and means of implementing the aims of the three items. The eight steps are *ge-wu* (格物)[13], extension of knowledge

(致知), sincerity of the will (诚意), rectification of the mind (正心), cultivation of the personal life (修身), regulation of the family (齐家), national order (治国), and world peace (平天下).

In fulfilling the aims of the three items, the eight steps are even more concrete and specific. There have been some disagreements regarding how the first step, *ge-wu,* should be interpreted. Zhu Xi (1130-1200 A.D.) took it to mean the investigation of principles (理), the laws of being, as inherent in things of the external world. This is the only way to make one's will sincere. On the other hand, Wang Yang-ming (Wang Shou-ren, 1472-1529 A.D.) considered principle to be inherent in the mind. Therefore, *ge-wu* does not mean to investigate principles inherent in things, but to correct what is wrong in the mind so as to preserve its inherent principle. On the basis of this argument, Wang criticized Zhu Xi for shifting the original chapters of the *Great Learning* so that the chapter on *ge-wu* appears before that on the sincerity of the will. Wang believed that the chapter on the sincerity of the will must come first. It seems to us that Wang's interpretation is more consistent with the three items of the *Great Learning* and the abovementioned opening statements of the *Doctrine of the Mean.* According to these two works, Confucian moral cultivation tends to nourish what is within and then gradually extend these internal moral values to external human relationships. The extension of knowledge for Wang is the extension of innate knowledge of the good (致良知).

With this interpretation, we can consistently claim that the first four steps lead to the fifth step, 'cultivation of personal life'. Hence all the five steps purport to fulfill the aim of the first item, i.e. manifesting the clear character of man. Similarly the last three steps, regulation of the family, national order, and world peace, are meant to fulfil the aim of the second item, 'loving the people'. When one has successfully manifested his clear character and fully extended his love to people, he has abided in the highest good. Therefore to be a Confucianist is to achieve these goals specifically spelled out above. All the other teachings of Confucianism are nothing but further elaborations upon these goals. For a Confucianist to achieve peace and order throughout the world, he must first of all cultivate his personal life.

To Confucius, a morally uncultivated person can never serve society. Because the superior man is like the wind and the vulgar

9

person (the commoner) is like the grass; in whichever direction the wind blows, the grass will bend. This Confucian political philosophy is fundamentally based upon Confucian moral philosophy. We have mentioned previously that the Confucian theory of education also has its foundation in the Confucian moral philosophy. Therefore, the Confucian moral philosophy, which can be summarized as manifesting the Heaven-bestowed moral character of man, is the foundation of Confucian orthodoxy.

In the *Great Learning* and the *Doctrine of the Mean,* Confucianism had already come a long way from the Master's fragmentary moral admonitions in the *Analects.* We have to wait until Mencius for a more penetrating and detailed treatment of the Heaven-bestowed moral character of men, i.e. human nature. Although Xun Zi also treated the problem of human nature, his naturalistic temperament precluded him from accepting the idea of Heaven as the source of human nature. Hence, Mencius has been regarded as orthodox due to his agreement with the above interpretations of Confucius as presented in the *Great Learning* and the *Doctrine of the Mean.* For his conflict with these interpretations, Xun Zi has been, fairly or unfairly, ostracized from the orthodox fold of Confucianism.

Mencius was famous for his theory of the goodness of human nature. With this theory, he not only continued but also further developed the orthodox view that human nature is fraught with moral qualities. The orthodox view as conveyed in the *Doctrine of the Mean* only reveals that we receive our nature from Heaven, and that when we follow this nature we shall attain morality. Yet, prior to Mencius, there had never been any discussion regarding what the moral components of this nature are, how the relationship between the mind (or heart) and this nature can be established, and finally how to prove the view that human nature is moral in content. For the first time, Mencius probed all these topics. He specifically analyzed the moral components of human nature in the following way:

A man without the heart (*Xin* 心) of commiseration is not a man; a man without the heart of shame and dislike is not a man; a man without the heart of deference and compliance is not a man; and a man without the heart of right and wrong is not a man. The heart of commiseration is the beginning of humanity (*ren* 仁); the heart of shame and dislike is the beginning of righteousness (*yi* 义); the heart of deference and compliance is the beginning of propriety (*li* 礼); and the heart of right and wrong is the beginning of wisdom (*zhi* 智).[14]

In Mencius' view, these 'four beginnings' are the inborn moral qualities of man and therefore the moral components that make up human nature. If properly nurtured they can grow and develop into the four virtues, i.e. humanity (*ren*), righteousness (*yi*), propriety (*li*), and wisdom (*zhi*).

Although Mencius' major thesis concerned the goodness of human nature, he could only discuss it indirectly through the human heart (taken in the moral sense). For instance, he tries to prove this thesis through the heart of commiseration. As human nature is something non-empirical, he had to grasp it through *xin* (human heart), which is closer to the empirical level. So it is important to know the relationship between *xin* and *xing* (human nature). *Xin* can be translated in English either as 'mind' or 'heart'. When translated as 'mind', it is understood as a cognitive entity. On the other hand, when translated as 'heart', it is considered as a moral entity.

Generally speaking, Mencius emphasized the moral aspect of *xin*, whereas Xun Zi focused upon its cognitive side. This explains the above translation of the Mencian *xin* as 'heart'. Human heart for Mencius is the manifestation of human nature as a metaphysical entity. Therefore, the former is the latter's link or 'point of contact' with the outside world. How do we know that man's nature is good? In Mencius' view, we know this because we are aware that every man without exception has the heart of commiseration. When we suddenly see a child about to fall into a well, we have the feeling of sympathy and compassion. This, for Mencius, constitutes the proof that man's nature is originally good. He had no doubt that the only way to assess man's nature is through his heart.

In the above quotation, when Mencius referred to the four different hearts, he meant the four different moral aspects of *xin*. In fact, he called them 'four beginnings' (四端) rather than 'four hearts'. It would be awkward indeed to say that man has four hearts. He further indicated that these four beginnings are in a sense the embryos of the four virtues: humanity, righteousness, propriety, and wisdom. And the embryos of the four virtues are qualitatively no different from the four virtues. Therefore, when we search into the contents of human heart (*xin*), we find nothing but moral ingredients, which can nourish the four virtues.

As human nature expresses itself in terms of human heart, the former can also be said to display itself through the four virtues. Can we go one step further by maintaining that human nature thus consists of the four virtues? On the surface, this does not seem to be a logical step. But if we consider the fact that human nature for Mencius is a metaphysical entity, we might be able to do so in a loose sense. For otherwise we can never describe the components of human nature. Or perhaps we are more comfortable with the mere reference of it in terms of its manifestations. But then it is a mere verbal disagreement.

Mencius further said, "He who exerts his heart (*xin*) to the utmost knows his nature. He who knows his nature knows Heaven. To preserve one's heart and to nourish one's nature is the way to serve Heaven...."[15] Here Mencius provided a metaphysical ground for man's moral efforts, which is consistent with the ortho- dox principles laid down in the *Great Learning* and the *Doctrine of the Mean.* Consequently, the heart, the nature, and Heaven are interrelated. If he preserves his heart, he will certainly nourish his nature and serve Heaven. Mencius considered it the aim of learning to recover the lost heart.

We have said that the concept of *ren* occupies the central position in Confucius' philosophy to the extent of being equivalent to the substance of morality. In the case of Mencius, although the dominant position of *ren* remains the same, it appears in a different context and receives a more philosophical treatment. For instance, in discussing the four beginnings we have quoted Mencius as saying that the heart of commiseration is the beginning of *ren* and the exertion of this heart can lead one to know both one's nature and Heaven. Furthermore, *ren* in its broad sense includes not only the heart of commiseration, but also the other moral aspects of *xin.*

In Mencius' view, *ren* is what constitutes man, and that *ren* is man's *xin.* Here *ren* is not just one of the four virtues but is the sum total of them. It is in this sense that *ren* becomes identified with the moral heart and the defining characteristics of man. Consequently, *ren* is also the manifestation of human nature. *Ren* as an all-inclusive virtue was later much developed by the Neo-Confucianists. Cheng Hao (1032-1085 A.D.) during the Song dynasty said, 'The man of *ren* forms one body with all things without any differentiation. Righteousness, propriety, wisdom, and faithfulness are all (expressions of) *ren.* '[16]

We have previously mentioned that for Confucius conscientiousness and altruism are the two practical methods of implementing *ren.* They constitute what we call the principle of *zhong* and *shu,* which is generally interpreted as the way to practice *ren.* [17] This interpretation is based upon the following conversation in the *Analects:*

> The master said: "Shen (the personal name of Zeng Zi, one of his disciples), all my doctrines are linked together by one principle." "Very much so," replied Zeng Zi. When the master had left the room, the other disciples asked: "What did he mean?" Zeng Zi replied: "Our master's doctrines are nothing but *zhong* and *shu.* "[18]

If Zeng Zi's understanding is to be trusted, his above interpretation is certainly correct. But, according to another interpretation, it is *yi* (righteousness) that is the principle to practise *ren.* [19]

Yi in this view is the moral insight or perception, which recognizes the fitness of *ren* for a specific situation. This is consistent with what Confucius said in the *Doctrine of the Mean:* '*Yi* is what is proper (in a particular situation).' But it is also true that his disciples never asked about *yi* in the *Analects,* although they often queried *ren,* filial piety and government.

Our present approach here to resolve the problem of whether the principle of *zhong* and *shu* or the principle of *yi* is the way to practise *ren* is a compromise between the two. On the one hand, we do not like to hold the view that Zheng Zi, one of the ablest and most philosophical disciples, misunderstood Confucius. On the other, there is enough evidence to believe that *yi* is also the principle for practising *ren.*

The solution of this apparent dilemma lies in Confucius' main philosophical concern. As the principle of *zhong* and *shu* is easier to grasp than the principle of *yi*, it would be more expedient for a practical moral philosopher like him to emphasize the former. In applying *zhong* and *shu*, one simply asks oneself what one likes and dislikes, whereas in applying *yi* one must possess the moral insight regarding what is proper and improper in a particular situation. Yet *zhong* and *shu* in spite of this advantage are too concrete and specific to be inclusive enough. *Yi*, due to the apparent emptiness of its content, is more comprehensive in its application, even though it is a more difficult philosophical principle to understand.

The two principles are not as incompatible as they appear to be. In fact, when one applies *zhong* and *shu*, one usually hits upon what is proper or *yi* in most moral situations. As a result, the principle of *zhong* and *shu* is as sound as the principle of *yi* in moral application. It is only in philosophical analysis that the principle of *yi* appears to be more comprehensive and thus more satisfactory than the principle of *zhong* and *shu*.

It is not until Mencius that the philosophical importance of *yi* is made explicit. Mencius, due to his philosophical acumen and his need to refute the various rival doctrines which Confucius never encountered, combined the philosophical subtlety of the *Doctrine of the Mean* and Confucius' concern for concrete moral implementations. He approached the moral substance of *ren* from a new perspective, i.e. the conjunction of *ren* with *yi*. Since *ren* is such a comprehensive concept, he must bring in another equally comprehensive principle of guidance for its actual application. The old principle of *zhong* and *shu* was adequate enough as far as guiding mere moral maxims was concerned, but not adequate enough to confront the more subtle philosophical attacks of his contemporary rivals. For example, his philosophical debate with Gao Zi (告子) on human nature is a case in point. The significance of *ren* and *yi* in conjunction can be explained in this following Mencian passage:

> *Ren* is man's *xin* (heart), and *yi* his path. It is sad indeed that some people would abandon their path without following it and that they would lose their *xin* without knowing how to retrieve it. When they lose their chickens and dogs, they know how to recover them, but not when they have lost their *xin*. The purpose of learning is nothing but getting back the lost *xin*.[20]

14

Here *yi* is the path for following *ren* and therefore the principle for applying *ren*. *Yi* provides moral insight and guidance as to how to adopt the most appropriate response to particular moral situations, which fits in well with the above-mentioned statement, '*Yi* is what is proper (in a particular situation).' *Yi*, for Mencius, is derived from the heart or feeling of shame and dislike. It is then developed to the extent that there is something one cannot bring himself to do (*you-suo-bu-wei* 有所不为).[21] Finally, *yi*, when properly and fully cultivated, will lead to *hao-ran-zhi-qi* (浩然之气), some sort of metaphysical flooding breath, which can fill up all between heaven and earth.

Our above discussions of *ren* and *yi* show the continuing development from Confucius through the *Great Learning* and the *Doctrine of the Mean* to Mencius. It is particularly through the interpretations of the *Great Learning* and the *Doctrine of the Mean* that we are able to recognize the obvious continuity between Confucius and Mencius. Without these interpretations we are not sure whether Mencius was in fact a more genuine representative of Confucius than Xun Zi, although Mencius has generally been considered to carry the orthodox line of transmission at the expense of Xun Zi. We shall next discuss Xun Zi, the last of the three major Pre-Qin Confucianists.

The uniqueness of Xun Zi's philosophy illustrates that Confucianism is not purely a fixed set of doctrines initiated by Confucius and handed down from generation to generation without much change. Even if Confucius' own philosophy can be said to be flexible enough to allow for the development of Xun Zi's ideas, many of these ideas are so revolutionary that they are diametrically opposed to the orthodox line of Confucianists. The uniqueness of Xun Zi lies in his 'naturalism' or 'positivism', which is a philosophical attitude to believe only in natural phenomena and positive facts regarding the origin of the universe without taking into account the supernatural and spiritual. In a way this is a further development of the humanistic spirit of Confucius. Unfortunately, this attitude was not employed to develop science.

To illustrate the naturalistic attitude of Xun Zi, let us study the following passages:

1 Heaven does not give up the winter because people dislike

cold. Earth does not give up its expanse because people dislike distance. The superior man does not give up good conduct because the inferior man rails against him.[22]

2 When stars fall or trees make a (strange) noise, all people in the state are afraid and ask, 'Why?' I reply: There is no need to ask why. . . . It is all right to marvel at them, but wrong to fear them. For there has been no age that has not had the experience of eclipses of the sun and moon, unreasonable rain or wind, or occasional appearance of strange stars.[23]

3 When people pray for rain, it rains. Why? I say: There is no need to ask why. It is the same as when it rains when no one prays for it.[24]

Here he nonchalantly dismissed the traditional belief of the unity between man and Heaven. Considering his cultural background, this attitude is truly revolutionary. The philosophical significance of this naturalistic temperament is twofold. First, it leads him to reject the view that human nature is bestowed by Heaven, and consequently to develop the theory that human nature is originally evil. Second, as the evil nature of man cannot be responsible for initiating moral standards, to cultivate moral values is a matter of imposing them upon man from an external source. As a result, the external rules of propriety (*li*) are what is important in shaping a moral person. These two points are the most important consequences of Xun Zi's philosophical naturalism, which we shall next investigate.

Unlike Mencius, Xun Zi, because of his naturalistic temperament, refused to become embroiled in metaphysics in his discussions of human nature. He provided some positivistic arguments for the evilness of human nature. We shall introduce here only one argument that has far-reaching philosophical implications upon the other aspects of his philosophy. He argued that man feels the desires of ears and eyes, which prompt him to crave for sound and beauty. If these tendencies are followed, strife and disorder will result.

This naturalistic interpretation of human nature on the basis of desires is diametrically different from Mencius' metaphysical approach. The difference between the two Confucianists is a matter of diverse approaches. Since they did not agree upon what human nature is, they naturally came to different conclusions regarding its characteristics. Regarding Xun Zi's pôsition, we are certainly well aware of the destructive nature of desires and passions. We do bar our doors at night and lock up our valuables, don't we? Do we not here as much accuse mankind by our actions as we would do by our words?

In attempting to resolve the difference between Mencius and Xun Zi, we should avoid treating them as proposing two incompatible theories regarding human nature. It is a disagreement over the nature of morality, which in turn leads to a disparity regarding the method of moral cultivations. Mencius was primarily interested in the moral ideal of how man ought to behave. When he further identified human nature with this moral ideal which is transcendental in origin, human nature could not but be good. Xun Zi, on the other hand, proposed to assess human nature on the basis of the actual manifestations of desires and passions, and thus arrived at an opposite view of human nature.

Consequently, Mencius' proposed method of moral cultivation is for man to bring out this moral ideal in daily conduct, whereas Xun Zi's approach is to rectify and regulate the destructive nature of desires through the imposition of external moral standards, i.e. the rules of propriety (*li*). Hence Xun Zi's belief in the evilness of human nature logically leads to his concept of *li* as social norms to set degrees and limits among people. Nevertheless he was not as concerned as Mencius with the internal process of moral cultivation.

In studying Xun Zi's concept of *li*, let us consider the following passage:

> What is the origin of *li*? I reply: Man is born with desires. If his desires are not satisfied for him, he cannot but seek some means to satisfy them himself. If there are no limits and degrees to his seeking, then he will inevitably fall to wrangling with other men. From wrangling comes disorder and from disorder comes exhaustion. The ancient kings hated such disorder, and therefore they established *li* and *yi* to distinguish things properly, to train men's desires and to provide for their satisfaction. They saw to it that desires did not over-extend the means for their satisfaction, and material goods did not fall short of what was desired. Thus both desires and goods were looked after and satisfied. This is the origin of *li*. [25]

17

First of all, *li* and *yi* were established by the ancient sage kings and not innate in human nature as in Mencius' system. Second, as people within a society seek to satisfy their desires, disorder often results. Third, *li* and *yi* were established to curb this disorder through making proper distinctions.

Here *li* and *yi* are moral norms, which are derived from external sources and not from human nature. In fact, they are means of checking the disorderly character of human nature. In Mencius there is a harmonious relationship between moral values such as *li* and *yi* and human nature. It is now transformed into one of conflict and tension in the case of Xun Zi. Therefore, for Xun Zi, moral cultivation was no longer a matter of bringing out and developing what is originally within ourselves as in Mencius. It became a matter of learning the norms from the sages, which are in turn established in the individual through habituation. Finally, the cultivation of *li* and *yi* is made possible by the cognitive mind of man, which is possessed by every man.

Although *li* is the centre of Xun Zi's moral theory, he often used *li* in conjunction with *yi* just as *ren* for Mencius is frequently linked with *yi*. As mentioned previously, for Xun Zi *li* and *yi* are objective moral norms for rectifying human nature, whereas for Mencius *li* and *yi* are moral values originating from and thus in harmony with man's nature. Apart from this fundamental difference, *yi* for both thinkers plays the common role of guiding the practice and fulfilment of morality in general.

We have also described how *yi* for Mencius provides moral insight and guidance in order to adopt the most appropriate response to particular moral situations. Similarly, *yi* for Xun Zi sets limits, degrees, and distinctions in particular situations. In other words, what is in accordance with *li* (rules of propriety) in one situation may not be so in another situation. It is *yi* that directs one to draw the most proper distinctions in human conduct. *Yi* thus defined is the guiding principle for practising *li*. Here we can still recognize some coherence between Mencius' *yi* and Xun Zi's *yi* in spite of different origins.

We are now to conclude what we have discussed so far about Pre-Qin Confucianism, which in our view is the gateway to Confucianism. A clear understanding of Pre-Qin Confucianism is tantamount to understanding the essence of Confucianism. Our approach so far to Confucianism of this period is first of all to trace the orthodox line, which is a continuation and development of Confucius' doctrines on the basic of the interpretations of the *Great Learning* and the *Doctrine of the Mean* and which reaches culmination in Mencius. The main features of this orthodox line are the advocacy of moral cultivation from within the selfhood.

This is evident by the procedure of 'making the will sincere', 'rectifying the mind', 'personal cultivation', 'regulating the family and the state', and eventually 'peace and order throughout the world (the Chinese Kingdom)', so clearly spelled out in the *Great Learning*. The *Doctrine of the Mean* and *Mencius* charter within man himself an entirely new universe with profound ontological depth reaching all the way to Heaven, the metaphysical fountainhead. This idea of working from within does not stop with the self and must be externalized to social and political areas as outlined above. Nevertheless there is the tendency among Confucianists to glorify those eminent historical figures who had perfected their inner moral qualities, but had not achieved much both socially and politically.

Confucius' ideal sages such as the legendary emperors, Yao (尧) and Shun (舜), were models of 'sageliness within and kingliness without, (内圣外王). 'Sagelines within' (内圣) refers to people who have perfected their inner moral qualities, whereas 'kingliness without' (外王) describes those who have established significant social and political achievements. The orthodox line tends to attach more value to the sageliness within. Xun Zi, on the other hand, developed the heterodox line of Pre-Qin Confucianism through emphasizing the kingliness without.

It should be noted that, in spite of his being banished from the orthodox fold, Xun Zi was as much a Confucianist as Mencius. For, without the 'kingliness without', the 'sageliness within' cannot complete Confucius' ideal model of a sage. In fact, Xun Zi's belief in the evilness of human nature should not be interpreted as a contempt of man. On the contrary, his theory leads to the idea that morality is the result of human efforts and not something ready-made by God or Heaven..The evilness of man's nature would urge man to redouble his moral efforts, which is precisely what Confucius' humanism is all about. Viewed from this perspective, Xun Zi could perhaps be said to further develop Confucius' humanism in a way not done by Mencius. Therefore, the arbitrary division into orthodox and heterodox camps of Confucianism by later Chinese scholars was simply a 'judgment of history' not necessarily contemplated by the Master, the founder of the school.

If we look at Chinese history in depth, we will not underestimate the influence of Xun Zi. His philosophical verdict of the untrustworthiness of human nature has influenced many Chinese rulers to secretly cherish the 'reward and punishment' method of legalism, even though they might still pay lip service to the orthodox doctrines handed down from Mencius. In the sense that legalism has been an influential force in Chinese history, Xun Zi's philosophical impact has always been enormous. If Confucius' moral ideal is how to become a sage in the aforementioned sense, Mencius' 'inner sageliness' must be complemented by Xun Zi's 'outer kingliness' to accomplish this ideal. In the final analysis, to be a Confucianist is to constantly aspire after such a profound ideal.

2

Confucian Views on
Human Nature

Confucius said, "By nature men are alike. Through practice they have become far apart."[1] In A.C. Graham's view, this is not a philosophical but a sociological observation that men's natural tendencies are not as different as they appear when they are later conditioned by environment.[2] If this well-known Confucian statement is not to be taken philosophically, human nature as a philosophical problem first appeared during Mencius' time, the fourth century B.C. Since then human nature has become a perennial philosophical pre-occupation for the Confucianists, and, in a way, the single most important problem in the history of Chinese philosophy.

Fu Si-nian (傅斯年) pointed out that *xing*, which means 'human nature', did not exist in the Pre-Qin literature as an independent graphical character.[3] It was then simply a phonetic variation of *sheng* (生), which originally means 'inborn'. Yet the character *sheng* did not at first carry the meaning of *xing*. It was in the *Confucian Analects* that *sheng* began to take over the meaning of *xing*. Nevertheless, this new meaning of *sheng* was only partially developed therein. It was not until Mencius that 'human nature' was fully developed as a separate meaning for *sheng* for the first time.[4] Although we do now find the graphical character *xing* in the *Confucian Analects*, the *Book of Mencius,* and the *Xun Zi*, these are the results of revisions by Han scholars.[5] Fu's evidences based on statistical, contextual, and linguistic approaches have been so overwhelming that his thesis of revisions by Han scholars has been accepted by most scholars in this field.

For philosophical reasons I tend to agree with Fu that the graphical *xing* appeared for the first time in Han. If we can see that it was the graphical *sheng* rather than the graphical *xing* that appeared whenever the problem of human nature was discussed

21

during the Pre-Qin period, we can then better understand the famous statement by Gao Zi: 'What is inborn is called nature', and the resultant exchange between him and Mencius. In response to this statement by Gao Zi, Mencius asked: "When you say that what is inborn is called nature, is that like saying that white is white?"[6] For '(the graphical) *sheng* is (the graphical) *sheng* (but pronounced as *xing*)' is obviously parallel in form to 'white is white'. Hence Gao Zi was induced to answer 'yes'.

According to Graham, "The *xing* of a thing, then, is its proper course of development during its process of *sheng.*" And the proper course of development for man is living to a ripe old age in good health.[7] This non-philosophical usage of *xing* was first used by people who were primarily concerned with the proper way of living out their natural spans of life. Graham pointed out that Yang Zhu (杨朱) made the first attempt to formulate a philosophy out of this non-philosophical concept of *xing*. Yang taught that one should 'complete one's *xing* and protect one's genuineness and not involve oneself in risk to the body for the sake of other things (全性保真, 不以物累形)'[8]. It follows from this teaching that one should refuse to sacrifice a hair of one's body even for the benefit of the entire world. This egoism (为我) was strongly attacked by Mencius as a matter of defending Confucian moral principles.

I share Graham's view that man's nature (*xing*), as commonly understood during the fourth century B.C., conflicted with the Confucian principles of benevolence and righteousness. Confucians taught that there are things which are more important than life and that sometimes we should sacrifice our lives for the sake of moral principles. But the non-philosophical understanding of *xing* at that time was to live out one's natural life span by all means. It was no wonder that common people flocked to Yang Zhu for a philosophy more congenial to their thinking. As Graham puts it:

> That man's unalterable nature is his endowment from Heaven is a point which a Confucian could not gainsay, since everything outside human control belongs by definition to the sphere of Heaven. But if Heaven is on the side of Yang Zhu, to what authority is a Confucian to appeal?[9]

This ideological sense of insecurity prompted Mencius to remark that 'the words of Yang Zhu and Mo Di (墨翟) fill the world. If the people in their opinions do not follow Yang Zhu, they follow Mo Di.'[10] Since then the ideological ghost of Yang Zhu has haunted the Confucianists for over two thousand years. When Xun Zi advocated that man's nature is originally evil, which smacks of Yang Zhu, he was soon ostracized from the Confucian orthodoxy. With the background of the problem of human nature presented above in mind, we can then evaluate the Confucian views on human nature in a proper historical perspective and feel the urgency of the problem from the Confucian point of view. We shall here focus upon three Confucian views on human nature as held by Mencius, Xun Zi, and Zhu Xi. Their views almost cover the whole range of Confucian discussions of the problem in the history of Chinese philosophy.

We now start with Mencius. As has been mentioned, the problem of human nature emerged as a primarily philosophical preoccupation for the Confucianists for the first time during the fourth century B.C. Furthermore, the non-philosophical origin of *xing* shows that Gao Zi's two statements 'what is inborn is called nature'[11] and 'by nature we desire food and sex'[12] were already prevailing assumptions at that time, which even Mencius himself would admit. The famous debate between Mencius and Gao Zi as recorded in the *Book of Mencius* was probably the first serious philosophical debate of the problem in the history of Chinese thought. The fact that Gao Zi was once a disciple of Mencius and respected by the latter (Mencius admitted that Gao Zi managed to maintain an unperturbed mind much earlier than he)[13] indicates that the issue of the debate was taken rather seriously.

In this interchange, Mencius seemed to gain the upper hand through skilfully manipulating Gao Zi's arguments to serve his own purpose. Yet, we are not so much persuaded by Mencius' arguments as by his power of eloquence. For instance, when he asked Gao Zi, ". . . must you violate the nature of the willow tree before you can make the cups and bowls?", he deliberately chose strong words like *qiang zei* (戕賊) (translated in the above quotation as 'violate'), which led to the inevitable conclusion that one must violate human nature in order to make it into humanity and righteousness.[14] Why didn't he instead use a neutral word or term meaning 'change' which would equally be consistent with Gao Zi's original argument?

D.C. Lau correctly points out the logical consequences of the assumption that one must violate human nature in order to imbue it with humanity and righteousness. The assumption itself is in fact a moral judgement. Since Gao Zi's position was that human nature is amoral, i.e. neither good nor bad, it would be unnatural for himself to make such a moral judgement. As Gao Zi made no comment on this assumption drawn by Mencius, we can only conjecture, Prof. Lau suggested, that Gao Zi must have accepted it. Yet Gao Zi's view that human nature is amoral does not allow him, logically speaking, to accept this assumption which is itself a moral judgement.

In other words, if man is in fact amoral by nature it would be unnatural for him to make a moral judgement like this. On the other hand, if, in interpreting Gao Zi's analogy of the willow tree, Mencius simply said that one must change human nature in order to imbue it with humanity and righteousness, then, in my opinion, the result would not be a moral judgement, which would be more consistent and thus less damaging to Gao Zi's position. In using words like *qiang zei,* Mencius was in a way passing his own moral judgement, which was not necessarily a corollary of Gao Zi's analogy.

Another analogy put forward by Gao Zi was this:

> Man's nature is like whirling water. If a breach in the pool is made to the east it will flow to the east. If a breach is made to the west it will flow to the west. Man's nature is indifferent to good and evil, just as water is indifferent to east and west.[15]

Mencius immediately objected to this, and then submitted his own version of the analogy: "Water, indeed, is indifferent to the east and west, but is it indifferent to high and low? Man's nature is naturally good just as water naturally flows downward."[16] The above interchange shows Mencius' skill in interpreting the analogy of water in such a way as to suit his own position. He was more interested in refuting Gao Zi's arguments for the theory

24

of amoral human nature than in *proving* his own view. Neither was Gao Zi interested in *proving* his view that human nature is neither good nor bad. His two analogies only served to *illustrate* rather than *prove* his view. Since analogies are never perfect, he was obviously at a disadvantage as far as the debate is concerned for first proposing them. It is due to this that although Mencius seemed to have won the debate, Gao Zi may have won popular sympathy.

Mencius' proof of the goodness of human nature, if any, can only be found in his discussion of the Four Beginnings. Since human nature consists of the Four Beginnings, proof of the latter would also amount to proof of the former. But, even so, he had only proven the First Beginning, e.g. the feeling of commiseration. It is hard to say whether Mencius here meant to prove the goodness of man's nature. It is possible that he might not be as concerned with proving the theory as with laying out its ethical and political implications. For instance, immediately before his discussion of the Four Beginnings, there is this passage:

> All men have the mind which cannot bear (to see the suffering of) others. The ancient kings had this mind and therefore they had a government that could not bear to see the suffering of the people. When a government that cannot bear to see the suffering of the people is conducted from a mind that cannot bear to see the suffering of others, the government of the empire will be as easy as making something go round in the palm.[17]

And after his discussion of the Four Beginnings, he ended with this:

> If anyone with these Four Beginnings in him knows how to give them the fullest extension and development, the result will be like fire beginning to burn or a spring beginning to shoot forth. When they are fully developed, they will be sufficient to protect all people within the four seas (the world). If they are not developed, they will not be sufficient even to serve one's parents.[18]

25

This context clearly indicates that Mencius was more concerned with showing the ethical and political implications of the Four Beginnings than with proving the Four Beginnings themselves. Other than the case of 'a child about to fall into a well', there is very little proof of the goodness of human nature in *Mencius*. He did not even try to prove the other three Beginnings along the same line as he did with the feeling of commiseration.[19]

In Xun Zi's theory of human nature, we find a more systematic account of the problem than in Mencius. One of his arguments for the original evilness of human nature goes like this. Man has the desires of ear and eye, which prompt him to crave for sound and beauty. If these tendencies are followed, strife and disorder will result. Guo mo-ruo (郭沫若) criticizes this as failing to understand the unique characteristics of man not possessed by other animals.[20] Guo also asks two pointed questions: "If man were from evil by nature, how would we explain the origin of goodness, propriety, or righteousness? If they were supposed to be invented by the sages, were the sages not also men like us?"[21]

Xun Zi also has this argument for man's evil nature. Psychologically, if one does not have it himself, he will seek it outside; if he has it himself, he will not seek it outside. For instance, if a man is ugly, he wants good looks. If poor, he desires to be rich. On the other hand, if a man is already handsome, he will not crave for good looks. If he is already rich, he will not pursue more wealth. Since people in general desire to be good, according to this line of argument, they must already have suffered from the lack of goodness in their nature. Therefore, it is clear that man's nature is originally evil.

Guo mo-ruo criticizes this second argument as the weakest among Xun Zi's arguments for the evilness of human nature. There is less objection, he says, against the principle that if one does not have it himself, he will seek it outside, but it is still possible to find exceptions to it. As to the principle that if he has it himself he will not seek it outside, Xun Zi himself should have known the untruth of it. Is it true that if a man is already rich he will not pursue more wealth? How many men of this kind can we find in the world? Guo then questions the validity of using this half truth as the major premise for deducing the original evilness of human nature.

Both Mencius and Xun Zi accepted the need for sage-kings

and morality in their theories. But their justifications for the need are different. For Mencius, moral efforts should be oriented towards 'developing one's nature', because man's original nature is already good. To him, the sage-kings are the paradigms of 'developing one's nature' to the utmost. It is in this sense that the sages are needed. Morality is needed because it is inherent in man's nature. For Xun Zi, moral efforts should be directed towards 'rectifying one's nature', because man's original nature is evil. The sage-kings can help man 'rectify his nature' through instituting morality. In other words, the sage-kings are needed for rectifying man's evil nature. From this analysis, we can see that the need for sage-kings cannot be used to deduce the evilness of human nature for it can equally be used to deduce Mencius' theory. When Xun Zi argued along this line, the argument was clearly invalid.

In my view, Xun Zi's strongest argument lies in his stress on the destructive nature of desires and passions. If anyone has any doubt about the destructive nature of desires, he has only to observe, Hobbes would say, what actually happens even in an organized society. He does bar his door at night and locks up his valuables. 'Does he not there as much accuse mankind by his actions, as I do by my words?' asked Hobbes. There is one statement by Xun Zi which is worth considering: "By nature man departs from his primitive character and capacity as soon as he is born, and he is bound to destroy it. From this point of view, it is clear that man's nature is evil".[22]

It would be interesting to know what this primitive character (朴) and capacity (资) is. This characteristic of man is something which is even more primordial than human nature, and which exists even before human nature can be determined. He used this primitive character and capacity not only to explain his view that man's nature is evil, but also to interpret Mencius' view that human nature is good. He said:

> By the original goodness of human nature is meant that man does not depart from his primitive character but makes it beautiful, and does not depart from his original capacity but utilizes it, so that beauty being (inherent) in his primitive character and goodness being (inherent) in his will are like clear vision being inherent in the eye and distinct hearing being inherent in the ear.[23]

The significance of this primitive character and capacity is that perhaps after all Xun Zi and Mencius were talking on different levels when they discussed human nature. This conjecture is in perfect agreement with the Neo-Confucian solution of the controversy between the two. According to the Neo-Confucians, 'human nature' can either refer to the essential nature (本然之性) or the physical nature (气质之性). The essential nature consists of the principles of humanity (*ren*), righteousness (*yi*), propriety (*li*) and wisdom (*zhi*), which are bestowed by heaven. In discussing man's nature, Mencius referred to the essential nature and therefore came to the conclusion that the nature of man is originally good. Xun Zi, on the other hand, referred to the physical nature which is the same essential nature conditioned by material force. Material force for the Neo-Confucians covers aroused feelings and desires. As he further emphasized desire as a fundamental characteristic of human nature, it follows that man's nature is evil to him. Moreover, the fact that he put man's nature in the same category as vision and hearing, which in his view cannot be learned, shows his determination to treat the problem empirically. And treating human nature empirically can never lead to the essential nature, at least from the Neo-Confucian point of view.

As we now touch upon the point at issue between Mencius and Xun Zi, we should avoid the temptation of treating them as offering two incompatible views, which would be philosophically most unprofitable. D.C. Lau suggests that we should consider them as disagreeing over the nature of morality, which in turn leads to a difference in the method of moral education, rather than a case of if one is right the other must be wrong and vice versa.[24] This to me is the most illuminating perspective to be taken before any discussion of the issue can be fruitful.

Lau offers the following interpretation of Mencius' theory: 'Now we see that Mencius' justification does not at all lie in the actual way in which human beings behave, but in the fact that they possess a sense of morality and a sense of shame.'[25] To say that man has a sense of morality, according to Lau, amounts to saying that he not only draws the distinction between right and wrong, but also approves of the right and disapproves of the wrong. The fact that man often does wrong cannot in any way invalidate Mencius' theory.[26] Then Lau poses this question: "Under what circumstances would we be entitled to say, in the same sense in which Mencius says that human nature is good, that human nature is bad?"[27] Lau then answers his own rhetorical question in the following way which, due to its importance, I now quote in full:

> We have seen that it would not do just to point out that human beings do very often act contrary to their duties. Man would need to approve of the wrong as such and feel ashamed of doing the right as such. But this would be a contradiction in terms, for when we approve of anything we do so because it is right, and when we disapprove of anything we do so because it is wrong, and so if we try to say that we approve of a thing because it is wrong, we feel that either it is a contradiction in terms or that 'wrong' really does not mean wrong but right.[28]

In Lau's view, the only way to prove Xun Zi's theory would be to show that man does in fact 'approve of the wrong as such and feel ashamed of doing the right as such.' By implication, Mencius' way of looking at morality makes better sense than Xun Zi's. Yet this line of argument by Lau presupposes a universal or Kantian standard of right or wrong. The divergence of moral theories in the history of ethics shows that any semblance of consensus as to right and wrong is still lacking. The Mencian example of a child about to fall into a well is only one of those few cases where some sort of moral consensus could be reached.

But if Lau means to say that one always approves *what he thinks is right,* this position of moral relativity has already departed from the main thrust of Confucian ethics. To avoid this difficulty, it would be philosophically more profitable to leave the issue open as Lau elsewhere suggests, viz. regarding the difference between Mencius and Xun Zi as a disagreement over the way of looking at morality. Otherwise, we might as well turn to the Neo-Confucian solution which after all is within the main Confucian context.

The importance of Song Neo-Confucianism cannot be over-emphasized. There were the so-called Five Masters of the early Song dynasty, i.e. Zhou Dun-yi, Cheng Hao, Cheng yi, Zhang Zai, and Shao Yong. It would go beyond the intended scope of this book just to summarize their respective views on human nature.

Since Zhu Xi has generally been regarded as a great synthesiser of their philosophies, we are now to probe his view on this subject as representing the prevailing view of this period. To open our discussion, let us consider the following passage by Cheng Yi:

> The nature is the same as principle. Traced to its source, none of the principles in the world is not good. Before they are aroused, have pleasure, anger, sorrow, and joy ever been found to be not good? As they are aroused and attain due measure and degree, they are good, no matter in what connection. When they are aroused and do not attain due measure or degree, then they are not good.[29]

Thus it is clear that, according to Cheng Yi, human nature is as Mencius stated, i.e. it is good. Zhu Xi generally followed this line of argument in his discussions of human nature. Yet for the first time the Song philosophers established a link between man's nature and principle (*li*).[30] By relating human nature with the concept of principle and tracing its metaphysical origin to the Supreme Ultimate (太极), they not only provided the metaphysical basis for Mencius' original goodness of human nature, but also resolved the controversy between Mencius and Xun Zi through distinguishing the 'essential nature' from the 'physical nature'.

As the two concepts of principle and material force are crucial in the Neo-Confucian treatment of the problem of human nature, Zhu Xi's greatest contribution lies in his distinction between the 'essential nature' and the 'physical nature', which is based upon these two concepts. Briefly speaking, the 'essential nature' consists of the four ethical principles of humanity, righteousness, propriety, and wisdom. These four principles of man correspond to the four principles behind the operation of the universe, i.e. *yuan* (元), *heng* (亨), *li* (利), and *zhen* (贞)[31] which in turn correspond to Spring, Summer, Autumn, and Winter respectively. What do all these relationships suggest in regard to the problem of human nature? Once it is assumed that man is somehow related to the principles of the universe and eventually to its origin, i.e. Master Zhou Dun-yi's Supreme Ultimate, would anyone still doubt the original goodness of human nature? The implication of this metaphysical system is clear enough.

The essential nature can also be explained in terms of 'principle' and 'destiny' (命), and also the Decree of Heaven. In the *Doctrine of the Mean*, it is said: 'What we receive from Heaven is called human nature.' Gu Hung-ming (辜鸿铭) translated this passage as 'The ordinance of God is what we call the law of our being.' With regard to this, Zhu Xi said:

> Yi-chuan (Cheng Yi) said that destiny is that which is endowed by Heaven and nature is what things have received from Heaven. Principle is one. As endowed by Heaven in all things it is called destiny. As received by creatures from Heaven, it is called nature. The difference lies really in the different points of view.[32]

Here for Zhu Xi and Cheng Yi, destiny and nature (the essential nature) are the same entity looked at from different points of view.

Regarding the relation between the essential nature and the principle, Zhu Xi said: "(Cheng Yi said,) 'The nature is the same as principle.' In relation to the mind, it is called nature. In relation to events, it is called principle."[33] He further remarked: "The principle of life is called the nature."[34] So according to the above rendition by Gu, man's essential nature as discussed in *The Doctrine of the Mean* is the law of our being, which is consistent with Zhu Xi's view that man's essential nature is the principle of life which man receives from Heaven as a divine decree or destiny. If this is the case, is there any doubt as to whether man's nature is good or evil?

But since the term 'nature' can also refer to the 'physical nature', the problem is much more complicated than it first appears. With regard to the meaning of the 'physical nature', Zhu Xi had this to say:

> Material force cannot be called the nature or destiny. They exist because of it, that is all. When the nature and Heaven and Earth are spoken of, it refers to principle only; when the physical nature is spoken of, it refers to principle and material force combined. Material force is not to be referred to as nature or destiny.[35]

When he described the physical nature as principle and material

31

force combined, he did not mean that the physical nature is a separate nature from the essential nature, which is not the case. In reference to this, J. Percy Bruce said:

> It must not be supposed, however, that there are two natures, the Essential and the Physical. There is only one nature; that is, the Essential Nature. The Physical Nature is still the Essential Nature, but conditioned by the physical element.[36]

The difficult task here is how to distinguish the essential nature from the physical nature without implying two separate natures. Zhu Xi himself often used water as an analogy to describe these two different phases of human nature. For instance, he compared destiny to water flowing and human nature to water contained in a bowl. He further said: "A big bowl contains more water, whereas a small one contains less. The water in a clean bowl will be clear, whereas that in a dirty bowl will be turbid."[37] He also remarked: 'For example, the good nature is like water. The physical nature is as though you sprinkled some sauce and salt in it and it then acquired a peculiar flavour.'[38]

Just as flowing water can be individualized into water in a bowl, so destiny can be individualized into man's nature. This is the meaning of 'what we receive from Heaven is called human nature'. The essential nature (the good nature) is water qua water; the physical nature is water mixed with some foreign element, be it sauce or salt. Here we can see that the two can be distinguished from each other without implying that they are two separate entities. Pure water being conditioned by salt can become salty water. The latter in turn can be purified into pure water. As the essential nature still runs through the physical nature, so water qua water does not disappear in salty water. Though there is always some danger to argue by analogy, Zhu Xi's point here can nevertheless be driven home.

Zhu Xi also believed that before man's birth we can only talk about principle and not (human) nature. As soon as nature is mentioned, it is already a stage after birth when principle has been compounded with material force. At this stage, nature is no longer the original (essential) nature.[39] If so, one question may be asked: Is it possible for the essential nature not to be conditioned

32

by material force? When asked about man's nature and destiny, Zhu Xi gave the following reply:

> If those born wise are completely and perfectly good, material force is there as material force and principle is there as principle, without any connection between each other. In such cases, there is no need to speak of the physical nature. But in the cases of men inferior to those born wise, even the Principle of Nature is not deficient. Nevertheless it is tied up with material force.[40]

Those born wise possess only the essential nature. The question here is whether men inferior to those born wise also have the essential nature. It is true that the essential nature of those inferior men is tied up with and thus conditioned by material force, which constitutes the physical nature. Yet what is important is that their essential nature is not tied up with material force at *birth*. For that matter, everyone's essential nature is not tied up with and conditioned by material force *at birth*.

This was what Mencius meant when he said man's nature is originally good. But we should not go one step further arguing that, for Mencius, the essential nature would always remain clear of the influence by material force. To sum up Zhu Xi's position, by distinguishing the essential nature from the physical nature, he was able to uphold Mencius' theory without, in the meantime, ignoring the problem of evil as strongly implied in Xun Zi's theory. This was the most significant contribution to the Neo-Confucian treatment of the problem of human nature.

To conclude our discussion of the controversy between Mencius and Xun Zi, I would like to refer to an observation by Homer H. Dubs.[41] According to Dubs, historical injustice has been done to Xun Zi by deprecating the latter as being unorthodox, whereas Mencius' view on human nature has been hailed as the orthodox interpretation of Confucius' position. Since authority is clearly a strong theme in Confucius' philosophy, Xun Zi's evilness of human nature consistently implies the need for authority in the true Confucian sense. Dubs believes that Xun Zi's theory was more in line with this Confucian authoritarianism. Furthermore, Xun Zi was less fatalistic and more naturalistic than Mencius in his confidence in man's ability to overcome inherent human nature, which seems to be a more logical development of Confucius' humanistic spirit.

It is both illuminating and instructive for D.C. Lau to interpret Mencius' theory as meaning that human beings are capable of distinguishing right from wrong.[42] This proposal does put Mencius in a more passive position. But then a new problem arises. The old Socratic thesis, 'knowledge is virtue', may not be true. Yet it is legitimate to ask the question: Without moral knowledge how do we distinguish right from wrong? And we have yet to reach any consensus concerning moral theories. This means that although philosophically our understanding of Mencius has increased since his time, the plausibility of his theory still remains what it was more than two thousand years ago.

It is quite possible that Yang Zhu made the first attempt to formulate a philosophy out of the non-philosophical concept of *xing,* viz. the proper way of living out one's natural span of life. In a broad philosophical sense, Xun Zi's theory was developed in the direction of Yang's egoism. Their views are more empirical in approach and devoid of any unnecessary metaphysical colouring. Xun Zi has often been criticized for confusing feelings (情) with human nature. This criticism is valid only if we have a consensus of what human nature is, which is precisely the point at issue.

D.C. Lau's suggestion of treating Mencius and Xun Zi as offering two different ways of looking at morality is the right direction to be taken for the solution of the issue. Yet it seems to me that the Neo-Confucian proposal provides the most satisfactory solution within the Confucian context. With the help of a metaphysical system, Zhu Xi treated human nature as the principle of life, relating it to the principle of existence of each and every thing, and eventually tracing it to the divine origin of the universe, the Supreme Ultimate. He used the essential nature to testify the original goodness of human nature, and the physical nature to explain the degenerate aspect of human character. He upheld and argued for Mencius' position in a competent and admirable way.

3
The Confucian Concept of "Immortality" and Its Cultural Implications

Although the concept of 'immortality' can be taken in various forms, it is usually interpretated religiously and associated with the soul and life after death. Plato, for instance, believed that the soul has three parts, i.e. 'reason', 'spirit', and 'appetite'. The rational part of the soul is supposed to guide and control the spirited and appetitive parts. Before the Platonic soul suffers the misfortune of descending to this sensible world, it resides happily in Heaven, the world of Forms. After the 'fall', the soul is encaged in the body. At the end of physical existence, the soul either returns to Heaven or drifts from body to body depending on the state of harmony or disharmony between the different parts of the soul. Hence, in occidental culture, 'immortality' generally means the immortality of the soul with the connotation of a life after death.

The Confucianists, the mainstay of Chinese culture, do not believe in the transmigration or the immortality of the soul. Their own peculiar view of immortality is primarily non-religious and humanistic in nature. This view has been manifested in the down-to-earth attitude and pragmatic orientation of the Chinese people. In this chapter, I will examine and analyse this Confucian view of immortality and its cultural implications. As my present discussion is in the main based upon established traditional scholarship and original documents, my presentation of the Confucian view should be acceptable to most people who are familiar with the Confucian tradition.

There is however some possibility of disagreement regarding the cultural implications of this particular view. Even if we could agree on the interpretation of a certain concept, its possible impact upon the people in general is debatable. Before we set out to identify the cultural implications of this Confucian immortality, we must assume that Confucianism is the main stream of Chinese culture and any Confucian doctrine would inevitably leave a great imprint upon the cultural make-up of the people.

Nevertheless, it is not to be supposed that the underlying cultural implications of the Confucian view are applicable to various Chinese societies in the same way. It goes without saying that the Chinese in Singapore are vastly distinct from the Chinese in China, who have been strongly influenced by Maoism and Marxism. Yet it is of utmost importance to recognize that the cultural implications of any traditional outlook or perspective are valuable points of reference in studying those societies that are still more or less under the sway of that outlook. The cultural implications are particularly relevant to tradition-bound societies. It is with this in mind that the significance of these cultural implications should be appreciated.

I shall start with the Confucian view of immortality. When Zi-lu (子路), one of Confucius' most celebrated disciples, asked about serving spiritual beings, the Master replied: "If we are not yet able to serve man, how can we serve spiritual beings?" Asked about death, Confucius said, "If we do not yet know about life, how can we know about death?"[1] This agnostic and non-committal attitude set the tone for later Confucianists regarding spiritual and religious matters. Personal immortality being the primary concern of Confucian gentlemen is therefore not openly discussed.

In *Zuo Zhuan* (左传), a commentary on Confucius' *Spring and Autumn Annals* (春秋), it is stated:

> It is of primary importance to establish virtue (立德), of secondary importance to render meritorious service (立功), and of final importance to expound ideas in writing (立言). In spite of the lapse of long time, these three achievements are always lasting and unforgettable. These are what we call 'immortality'.[2]

Since *Zuo Zhuan* is one of the earliest Confucian Classics and the above quotation is consistent with the humanistic spirit of Confucianism, it is the first formulation of the Confucian view of immortality.

In the *Doctrine of the Mean* (中庸), a metaphysical basis is provided for this down-to-earth and humanistic approach to

36

immortality. It is stated in the opening paragraph of this work: "What Heaven has conferred upon man is considered human nature. To act in accordance with the moral dictates of human nature is the Way (Dao 道). The cultivation of the Way is what we call culture." This celebrated passage was later greatly capitalized by the Neo-Confucians from the eleventh century onwards. As each human being receives his nature, his law of being, from Heaven (the ultimate source of creation), to act in accordance with the moral dictates of human nature is the way to immortality. This is a metaphysical transformation of the original Confucian formulation of immortality in *Zuo Zhuan.*

But it must be noted that this immortality is not to be taken in the religious sense of life after death. It is still as earthly as establishing virtue, rendering meritorious service, and expounding ideas in writing, although all these are now interpreted with a metaphysical twist. But one fresh idea presented in the *Doctrine of the Mean* is that human nature now does not perish with the physical body. A new philosophical horizon has been opened to human nature, which now shares the divine qualities of Heaven and becomes as everlasting as Heaven. Therefore, on the one hand, immortality is to be sought in an earthly setting of following the moral dictates of human nature. On the other, since Heaven-conferred human nature is not limited to the life span of a perishable physical body, its immortality does have certain cosmic reality.

In another passage of the same work, Confucius said: "The life of the moral man is an exemplification of the universal moral order."[3] Through establishing virtue in this life, a person can be immortal because he exemplifies the universal moral order. The author of the *Doctrine of the Mean* believed that a person cannot be immortal through physical continuation or through the perpetuation of the soul, but through exemplifying the way, the universal moral order. As the Way can only be experienced by the person practising virtue, but cannot be verified empirically, the significance or insignificance of this argument largely hinges upon the individual's moral experience.

No other Confucianist is more confident of achieving immortality than Mencius. His confidence is clearly shown in his description of the 'strong, moving power (浩然之气)'. He had this to say about the power:

It is difficult to describe. As power, it is exceedingly great and exceedingly strong. If nourished by uprightness and not injured, it will fill up all between heaven and earth. As power, it is accompanied by righteousness and the Way. Without them, it will be devoid of nourishment. It is produced by the accumulation of righteous deeds but is not obtained by incidental acts of righteousness.[4]

Now, according to him, this strong, moving power will fill up all between heaven and earth. In making this statement, he would not believe that a man's life ends with his physical death. This strong, moving power is man's built-in link to immortality. Yet whether one preserves this power or not depends on the way it is nourished. It must be nourished by uprightness, righteous deeds, and, most of all, the Way. To follow the Way, according to the *Doctrine of the Mean,* is to act in accordance with the moral dictates, the four components of our human nature, i.e. humanity, righteousness, rules of propriety, and wisdom.

Mencius believed that man has the four inborn moral potentials, the four moral beginnings, to be developed into the above four virtues. This shows that in Mencius' view our everyday moral acts can nourish this mysterious, strong, moving power, which is man's only link with immortality. This earthly approach to immortality is rather consonant with Confucius' heritage. It should be borne in mind that this Mencian metaphysical theory serves only to philosophically justify the aforementioned four virtues, which are of the utmost importance to a Confucianist. Even for Mencius' metaphysical preference he was fundamentally a moral philosopher. And a Confucian moral philosopher's priority always lies in promoting the human welfare of this world.

Mencius also held that man in fulfilling his moral obligations as dictated by his nature is in a way performing Heaven-entrusted missions. Therefore doing one's moral duty well in this life carries a significance far beyond this mundane life, whether the well-performed duty is virtue (德), meritorious service (功), or ever-lasting writings (言). Consider this other passage by Mencius:

When Heaven is about to confer a great responsibility on any man, it will exercise his mind with suffering, subject his sinews and bones to hard work, expose his body to hunger, put him to poverty, place obstacles in the paths of his deeds, so as to stimulate his mind, harden his nature, and improve wherever he is incompetent.[5]

For Mencius it is Heaven that confers great responsibility upon man. Consequently, Heaven is as anxious as man to have the great responsibility successfully carried out. Due to Heaven's participation, a great responsibility well fulfilled will have an immortal quality.

Mencius' confidence in this immortality lies in his full awareness of the link between man and Heaven. Under the influence of the *Doctrine of the Mean*, he felt that this link is the very guarantee of man's immortality. He explicitly expressed his belief in this link thus: "He who exerts his mind to the utmost knows his nature. He who knows his nature knows Heaven. To preserve one's mind and to nourish one's nature is the way to serve Heaven."[6]

Although in the history of Confucianism there have been vacillations between naturalism and idealism, most Confucianists are quite consistent in their agnostic and sceptical attitude towards spiritual beings. Mencius, Lu Xiang-shan, and Wang Yang-ming are considered idealistic Confucianists not because they belived in spiritual beings, but because they emphasized the philosophical significance of the mind. The non-religious attitude towards spiritual beings is more strikingly shown in naturalistic Confucianists such as Xun Zi, Cheng Yi, and Zhu Xi. For instance, Xun Zi wrote:

> When stars fall or trees make a (strange) noise, all people in the state are afraid and ask, "Why?" I reply: There is no need to ask why. These are changes of Heaven and Earth, the transformation of *yin* (阴) and *yang* (阳), and rare occurrences.[7]

As a firm believer in rationality, Cheng often advised people to trust only what is conceivable. Once when someone talked about seeing a ghost, he asked:

> Did you see it with your own eyes? One should believe only in what one sees with one's own eyes. What is told as

39

a story is not worthy of credence. Even what one sees with one's own eyes may be caused by an ocular deficiency.[8]

There was also a record of this following dialogue:

> An inquirer after truth asked Cheng Yi: "Do ghosts and divinities have features?" The Philosopher replied: "Yes, they do." The questioner resumed: "If they have features, then it is certain that ghosts and divinities exist." Cheng Yi commented: "The so-called ghosts are transformations of the universe."[9]

What is significant about Cheng Yi's attitude towards spiritual beings is this: On the one hand, he advised that one should believe only in what one sees with one's own eyes; on the other, he had to compromise with the traditional belief by not rejecting outright ghosts and divinities, by maintaining that they have features. But when finally pressed to admit whether they exist or not, he answered ambiguously that they are 'transformations of the universe'. Basically, Cheng Yi, like most Confucianists, was against any reliance upon spiritual beings. For instance, he strongly objected to praying for rain and dew in the temples. His argument was: If mountains and rivers cannot make rain and clouds, how can idols effectively perform the job?

Zhu Xi, the great Neo-Confucian synthesizer, was equally ambiguous and even evasive regarding spiritual beings. When asked about them, he replied:

> How can this matter be quickly explained? Even if it could, would you believe it? You must look into all principles of things and gradually understand, and then this puzzling problem will be solved by itself.[10]

He once answered the same question with the following quotations from Confucius: "Devote oneself earnestly to the duties due to men, and respect spiritual beings but keep them at a distance. This may be called wisdom."[11] and "If we are not yet able to serve man, how can we serve spiritual beings?"[12] It is notable that almost seventeen hundred years after Confucius this attitude towards

40

spiritual beings and thus immortality remains more or less the same. The only variation in the case of Neo-Confucians is that under the ideological challenge of Buddhism they began to provide a metaphysical but rationalistic account of death, the soul, the cycle of birth and death, spiritual beings and the source of creation. But in their hearts they are both lukewarm and sceptical about spiritual beings. Fundamentally they are more interested in concrete moral problems which are matters of this worldly concern.

Neo-Confucians' more rationalistic account of spiritual beings is a far cry from the general masses' superstitious belief of them. To give an example, Zhu Xi said:

> All cases of material force which is coming forth belong to *yang* (阳) and are positive spiritual force. All cases of material force which is returning to its origin belong to *yin* (阴) and are the negative spiritual force.[13]

According to this explanation, the morning, the sun, plants growing, and a young man are positive spiritual force (*shen* 神), whereas the afternoon, the moon, plants declining, and an old man are the negative spiritual force (*gui* 鬼).

Zhu Xi gave an equally rationalistic interpretation of *hun* (魂) and *po* (魄), which are closely related to the above-mentioned *shen* and *gui*. In his view, *hun* as the heavenly aspect of the soul is composed of the clear part of material force, and *po* as the earthly aspect of the soul is composed of the turbid part of material force. Like *shen* and *gui, hun* and *po* belong to *yang* and *ying* respectively. Man's birth results from the integration of material force. When his material force becomes exhausted, he dies. At death the heavenly aspect of the soul returns to Heaven, whereas the earthly aspect of the soul returns to the Earth.

To sum up, it is Zhu Xi's belief that spiritual beings, the soul, birth, and death are nothing but the transformations of the universe. His account of death is reminiscent of the Taoist view that death is nothing but a transformation from one form of existence to another. And if human existence is the source of joy, why should death, another form of existence, be the source of sorrow? When Zhuang Zi's (庄子) wife died, he sang beating time on a bowl. His own justification of this uncanny behaviour was that life and death are like the alternations of the four seasons. They just follow a natural course, and therefore should never be causes for joy or sorrow.

Except for occasional eclipses as during the flourishing period of Buddhism, Confucianism had dominated the Chinese cultural scene until 1917, the beginning of the May Fourth Movement, which marked the first powerful and total attack on Confucianism. Although Confucianism lost much of its cultural influence after 1917 and was almost completely devoid of its influence after 1949 in China, its sceptical and agnostic attitude towards spiritual beings and life after death has left a permanent imprint upon the Chinese people.

There may still be some superstitious beliefs in ghosts and divinities among the less educated masses primarily owing to other religious influences. These lingering beliefs have become weaker and less prevalent because of the popularization of education and new knowledge. Most Chinese intellectuals clearly follow Confucius' dictate of 'respecting spiritual beings but keeping them at a distance'. As a result, Chinese intellectuals following the tradition of Confucius, Mencius, Xun Zi, Cheng Yi, and Zhu Xi are in general non-religious but not atheistic. They simply manage to keep a distance from spiritual beings.

With regard to Chinese intellectuals' non-religious approach to spiritual matters, Dr Hu Shi's (胡适) 'theory of social immortality (社会不朽论)'[14] is a case in point. It is a combination of the view that at death the soul will disperse and not retain its personal identity and the 'theory of the three kinds of immortality (三不朽)' as contained in *Zuo Zhuan*. He specifically referred to Fan Zhen (范缜) of South and North Dynasties (420-589 A.D.) regarding the latter's theory of the destructibility of the soul. According to Fan, the soul is nothing but the function of the physical body just as the sharpness of the knife is nothing but the function of the knife. Without the physical body or knife there is no soul or sharpness. Therefore for many Chinese intellectuals like Dr. Hu Shi, who believe in this theory, life after death in the sense of personal immortality is clearly out of the question.

The natural alternative is the Confucian 'theory of the three kinds of immortality' mentioned above. Yet in his view, there are three defects in this theory. First, immortality is only limited to those few people who have established exceptional virtues (such as legendary emperors Yao and Shun), glorious achievements (such as Great Yu (大禹), who solved the flooding problem in ancient China), and epoch-making writings (as those who left everlasting moral teachings). Second, immortality is limited only to positive but not negative deeds. For instance, if Columbus' discovery of America is immortal in the sense of constituting a glorious achievement, is Hitler's massacre of the Jews also immortal albeit in a negative sense? The third defect is its vagueness as to what kinds of virtue, achievement and writing are immortal.

According to Dr Hu's 'theory of social immortality', an individual's life at each moment is a 'small self (小我)', and his whole lifetime consists of many small selves including those of the past, the present, and the future. Each small self is influenced and caused by many small selves in the past, not only his own past small selves but also the small selves of his innumerable deceased ancestors and other ancients. The mutual influences of all these small selves are carried out in both historical and social dimensions. For example, small selves within the same society at a certain period of time can influence one another. These are mutual influences in the social dimension. And past small selves may influence present small selves, whereas present small selves may influence future small selves. These are mutual influences carried out historically.

The accumulation of all the innumerable small selves of the past, the present, and the future constitute the 'great self (大我)'. Every small self is perishable, but the great self is everlasting. The small self dies sooner or later, but what he has said, written and done, his merits or demerits, right or wrong, will be permanently retained in the great self. What the great self has recorded, not even pious sons and grandsons one hundred generations from now can alter. This is what Dr Hu called 'social immortality' or 'immortality of the great self'.

What is unique about this theory is that both merits and demerits, both great and small doings have their immortal qualities. One example given by Dr Hu is that if a tubercular person spits on the road and passes on germs to another person who then contracts the disease and in turn communicates to members of his family, even long after the first person dies, the effects of his careless action will still remain. In this sense, what he has done is immortal in a negative sense. Although Dr Hu was known for his leading role in anti-Confucian activities during the May Fourth Movement, his theory of social immortality was clearly influenced by the Confucian view of immortality, particularly the afore-mentioned 'three kinds of immortality', and the Confucian scepticism of the religious soul or personal immortality. With the support of the powerful Confucian tradition, Dr Hu's theory has been well received by Chinese intellectuals in general and, in my opinion, will eventually prevail among Chinese people.

To conclude, we would like to draw three cultural implications from the Confucian view of immortality. These implications can be fruitfully used as points of reference in sociological studies of many predominantly Chinese societies. The first cultural implication is religious apathy and tolerance. Religion has been less of an issue in Chinese culture than in any other culture. There were rarely religious persecutions in Chinese history. This apathy and tolerance have been manifested in various ways. In some Chinese temples, Taoist gods, Buddhist gods, and even Confucius deified as a god are worshipped under the same roof. It is not unusual for a Chinese to proclaim belief in more than one religion. This is unimaginable in a culture which takes religion more seriously. It is rather common in China for members of the same family to adopt different religions and to live peacefully with one another. Furthermore, if a Chinese has any objection to inter-racial marriage, cultural or even racial difference may be a consideration, but rarely the religious difference.

When Marxism was first introduced into China, significantly the initial hindrance to its acceptance was not its atheism but its variance with traditional culture. In 1977 Mr Lee Kuan Yew, the Prime Minister of Singapore, referring to the religious make-up of the new Members of the Singapore Parliament, said:

> There are 15 out of 69 (Members of Parliament) who swore on the Bible. Fifteen out of 69 is 21.75 per cent of the population of this House. . . . But in total population the Christians are only about 9 per cent. Twenty-one per cent in this House representing 9 per cent. I think the next time we introduce candidates we had better have a closer look.[15]

What puzzled Mr Lee is the fact that 21 per cent of the total MP's are Christians who represent only 9 per cent of Singapore's population. Since 77 per cent of Singapore's population are Chinese, religious apathy and tolerance may perhaps explain this fact. This would be unusual in predominantly Christian or Islamic countries, but nothing unusual in a predominantly Chinese society like Singapore. The Chinese, because of this cultural uniqueness, do not take religion seriously enough to vote along religious lines.

The second cultural implication is the this-worldly and humanistic philosophy of Chinese people. When a culture does not stress the belief in life after death, it is bound to pay more attention to this very life. Dr Lin Yutang described a Chinese pagan as 'one who starts out with this earthly life as all we can or need to bother about, wishes to live intently and happily as long as his life lasts.'[16] This description also suits a Confucianist rather well. For instance, Confucianists like Cheng Yi and Zhu Xi might affirm spiritual beings in terms of *yang* and *ying*, positive and negative spiritual forces, but would never allow spiritual beings to interfere with human activities. It is human efforts and not spiritual beings that are important.

Since, for a Confucianist, this life is all we have to be concerned about, what man should strive after is not the immortality of the soul, but the immortality of race and culture, and the three kinds of immortality (virtue, glorious achievements, and epoch-making writings) as improved and better expressed in Dr Hu Shi's theory of social immortality. This explains why the main concern of Confucianism lies in human relations and moral problems; why Chinese are this-worldly and achievement-oriented; and why they are concerned with the cultivation of one's virtue in order not to shame one's ancestors, and to pass on something of which his posterity may be proud. This is also why they esteem scholarship, the one enterprise most related to writing, which is one of the three ways of achieving immortality.

The third cultural implication is the belief in 'oneness between Heaven and man (天人合一)' to substitute institutional religions. A more detailed discussion of this important doctrine will be conducted in the next chapter. It suffices here to give a brief account of it. The ancient Chinese, being peasants, were very much impressed by the regular and orderly transformation of natural phenomena like the alternation of day and night, and the rotation of the four seasons which would determine their sowing and harvesting and thus have a strong impact upon their livelihood. Gradually there developed a belief that natural phenomena were inseparable from human affairs. This was later developed into the Confucian doctrine of 'oneness between Heaven and man.'

This doctrine has inspired many literary and philosophical writings throughout Chinese history. For instance, it has inspired the Neo-Confucian theory that the man of *ren* (humanity) regards Heaven and Earth and all things as one body. This theory is most excellently expressed by Zhang Zai in *The Western Inscription* (西铭):

> Heaven is my father and Earth is my mother, and even such a small creature as I find an intimate place in their midst.
>
> Therefore that which fills the universe I regard as my body and that which directs the universe I consider as my nature.
>
> All people are my brothers and sisters, and all things are my companions.[17]

This deep sense of union and harmony with the universe is in a way more fundamental and more satisfying, at least for Chinese intellectuals, than personal immortality or religious life after death.

Professor Qian Mu (钱穆) says that, while transcending religious theories, Confucianism manages to fulfill religious functions. To him, Confucianism does not look for God outside the human mind. A Confucianist would seriously believe that within the human mind there is a certain infinitude regarded by him as human nature. Just as religious thinkers seek for the highest good of God outside their own minds, so Confucianists seek for the highest good of human nature inside their own minds.[18]

Professor Qian further argues that, in spite of the lack of emphasis upon an external god, Confucianism contains all the inspiring sentiments and functions of an institutional religion.[19] These unique 'religious' sentiments for Confucianists could well substitute for institutional religions, which tend to prescribe a personal god pressurizing from outside. This is what it means when we say taht although Confucianism may not be considered a religion, it is by no means atheistic.

As far as the attitude towards 'spiritual forces' is concerned, the gap between the intellectuals and the masses has gradually been bridged through modern education and knowledge. I am confident that the intellectuals' attitude will eventually prevail upon the masses. Since Chinese intellectuals are greatly influenced by the Confucian view of immortality, it therefore has far-reaching cultural implications, which may serve as useful references in studying Chinese people and Chinese societies.

4

The Confucian Harmony and Union between "Heaven and Man"

This chapter attempts to expound the thesis that a methodological approach to Confucianism is still the most fruitful way of tackling the subject. In spite of the various complaints concerning the disconnectedness, the fragmentariness, and the amateurism of Chinese philosophy, we shall illustrate here how one principal doctrine in Confucianism can throw much light upon many seemingly unrelated Confucian problems. This doctrine is the 'oneness (harmony and union) between Heaven and man' (hereafter 'oneness doctrine'). The ancient Chinese were primarily peasants and, as peasants, they tended to watch closely the transformations of natural phenomena like the operations of four seasons, which regulated their sowing and harvesting and thus had a strong impact upon their livelihood. Gradually there developed a belief that natural phenomena were closely related to human affairs.

It was further developed into the thinking that the good or bad omens of the future could be predicted by experts through studying these natural phenomena. As a result, the aristocrats believed in always consulting these experts whenever they were about to engage in major events like expedition, hunting, or marriage. The oracle bones handed down from Shang dynasty are full of divination records. This belief was the origin of the oneness-doctrine, which has since then found a permanent place in the Chinese mind. Significantly Confucius himself was a descendant of the Shang people. Hu Shi even went as far as proclaiming that the Confucianists during Confucius' time were all descendants of this conquered people. As the term 'Heaven' is amenable to various interpretations as the sky, the totality of natural phenomena, moral being, anthropomorphic being, fate, and metaphysical entity, this oneness doctrine has undergone several evolutionary changes in the history of Confucianism.

This peasant-mentality-origin oneness doctrine is a truly philosophical fountainhead to which many Confucian theories can be traced back. This is the methodological consideration we have in mind in this essay. Consequently the importance of this oneness doctrine can not be over-emphasized. The doctrine can be found in the oracle bones, the 'Grand Norm' of the *Book of History,* the *Book of Changes,* the *Analects,* the *Doctrine of the Mean,* the *Book of Mencius,* the Yin-Yang School, the Yue Ling (月令) or 'Monthly Commands' as found in the *Lu Shi Chun Chiu* (呂氏春秋) and later embodied in the *Li Ji (Book of Rites),* in Dong Zhong-shu's Yin-Yang Confucianism, and, most important of all, in Neo-Confucianism.

The oneness doctrine does not remain the same in the various classical records and schools of thought, for even Confucianism itself has to undergo various phases of historical transformations. For instance, the doctrine as formulated by Dong Zhong-shu could not be found in Confucius. While Dong embraced the doctrine literally and superstitiously, Confucius took it philosophically by saying: "Does Heaven (*Tian*/Nature) say anything? The four seasons run their course and all things are produced. Does Heaven say anything?"[1] In other words, Confucius simply meant to say that the way Heaven operates can be emulated by man. The *Analects* shows that in moments of distress and despair he frequently referred to Heaven.

Roughly this oneness doctrine can be divided into the superstitious oneness and the metaphysical oneness. When the irrational elements of Confucianism gained ascendancy we had the former. When the philosophical temperament won the upper hand we had the latter. The Yin-Yang School and Yin-Yang Confucianism belong to the first category, whereas the *Doctrine of the Mean, Mencius,* and Neo-Confucianism except perhaps Shao Yong's philosophy belong to the second category. In a more exact analysis, the *Doctrine of the Mean* and *Mencius* have elements of both categories. One passage in the *Doctrine of the Mean* reads: "When a nation is about to flourish, there are sure to be happy omens; when it is about to perish, there are sure to be unluckly omens."[2] This, to a certain extent, still reflects the superstitious doctrine of 'the mutual influence and response between nature and man', propounded in the 'Grand Norm' and developed by the Yin-Yang school. For both the 'Grand Norm' and the Yin-Yang school maintain that 'bad conduct on the part of the sovereign results in the appearance of abnormal phenomena in the world of nature.'[3]

According to Feng You-lan, this mutual influence and response can be explained in either teleological or mechanical ways. The sovereign's bad conduct can cause Heaven to become angry and thus bring about abnormal natural phenomena as a warning from Heaven to the sovereign. This explanation is teleological. Or it can be explained that the bad conduct automatically disturbs the mechanical order of the universe and thus brings about abnormal phenomena. Feng You-lan maintains that the mechanical view represents the scientific spirit of the Yin-Yang school, while the teleological view reflects its occult origin.[4] It seems to me that any emphasis upon the scientific spirit of this 'mutual influence and response' tends to read too much into the original theory. I, on the contrary, maintain that the undue emphasis of the position of man in the universe by the oneness doctrine precisely runs against the objectivity of scientific spirit.

As a matter of fact, those Confucianists who were of naturalistic and scientific temperaments were apt to be rather sceptical of the oneness doctrine. For instance, Xun Zi, Yang Xiong, and Wang Chong (王充) explicitly attacked the doctrine. Xun Zi said:

> Nature (*Tian*/Heaven) operates with constant regularity. It does not exist for the sake of (sage-emperor) Yao nor does it cease to exist because of (wicked king) Jie. Respond to it with peace and order, and good fortune will result. Respond to it with disorder, and disaster will follow.[5]

In another passage:

> When stars fall or trees make a (strange) noise, all people in the state are afraid and ask, "Why?" I reply: There is no need to ask why. These are changes of heaven and earth, the transformation of *yin* and *yang*, and rare occurrences. It is all right to marvel at them, but wrong to fear them. For there has been no age that has not had the experience of eclipses of the sun and moon, unreasonable rain or wind, or occasional appearance of strange stars.[6]

And Wang Chong's scepticism of the oneness doctrine was even more uncompromising, when he wrote:

> Man holds a place in the universe like that of a flea or louse under a jacket or robe. . . . Can the flea or louse, by conducting themselves either properly or improperly, affect the changes or movements in the ether under the jacket? . . . They are not capable of this, and to suppose that man alone is thus capable is to misconceive of the principle of things and of the ether.[7]

In another passage, he said: "The Way of Heaven is that of spontaneity, which consists of non-activity. But if Heaven were to reprimand men, that would constitute action and would not be spontaneous."[8] In these quotations from Xun Zi and Wang Chong, there are clear scepticism and even open repudiation of the 'mutual response and influence between Heaven and man'. And Yang Xiong himself was also sceptical of the Mencian doctrine that every five hundred years a sage would arise. So it is clear that these naturalistic Confucianists would not consider this 'mutual response and influence' as scientific. Only idealistic Confucianists who, if not superstitious, were far less scientific than Xun Zi, Yang Xiong, and Wang Chong, believed in this doctrine.

We share Bertrand Russell's view that if there were a Being who could view the universe impartially, without the bias of *here and now,* he would hardly mention man, except perhaps in a footnote near the end of the volume.[9] What can at best be said of the Yin-Yang school is that there is the theoretical potential to be developed into the kind of oneness doctrine as found in Neo-Confucianism, which is called the metaphysical oneness doctrine in our above classification. It is true that some scholars like Dr Hu Shi do interpret Neo-Confucianism as representing the scientific spirit of China.[10] What Feng You-lan regards as the teleological view is considered by us here as the superstitious oneness doctrine owing to its primitive religious element which is not entirely rational and systematic. So we would consider the oneness doctrine of the 'Grand Norm' and the Yin-Yang school as fundamentally superstitious.

Although we have mentioned above the superstitious aspect of the *Doctrine of the Mean,* it contains this other passage: "What

Heaven (*Tian*/Nature) imparts to man is called human nature. To follow our nature is called the Way (*Dao*). Cultivating the Way is called education."[11] This particular passage had been repeatedly referred to by the Neo-Confucianists in their theories of human nature, which, in spite of the slight internal variations among them, constitute what we would call the metaphysical oneness doctrine. It is this aspect of the *Doctrine of the Mean* that leads us to consider it in a general classification as propounding a metaphysical oneness doctrine.

Mencius is another important source of inspiration for the Neo-Confucianists besides the *Doctrine of the Mean*. One of the most celebrated passages by Mencius is this: "He who exerts his mind to the utmost knows his nature. He who knows his nature knows Heaven. To preserve one's mind and to nourish one's nature is the way to serve Heaven. . . ."[12] This was later greatly capitalized by the Neo-Confucianists, and is clearly consistent with the metaphysical oneness doctrine. Yet Mencius also believed that every five hundred years there would emerge a sage emperor.[13] And since the interval between King Wen, the founding emperor of Zhou dynasty, and Confucius was about five hundred years, there was speculation among the more superstitious Confucianists that after all Confucius had the mandate from Heaven to be king, albeit an uncrowned king. This is why in our general classification we consider Mencius to have maintained a metaphysical oneness doctrine, although in a more exact classification what he proposed seems to contain elements of both kinds of oneness doctrine.

The oneness doctrine reached its culminating point in Neo-Confucianism when its irrational and superstitious elements gave way to rational and metaphysical considerations. And philosophically it is the latter that is more significant. The Neo-Confucianists were fortunate enough to be in a position to reap the philosophical harvest of all the previous developments of this oneness doctrine. To study the history of these developments is to study how Neo-Confucianism came into being. This is particularly true in the case of Neo-Confucian cosmology and metaphysical treatment of human nature.

We have so far explained the origin and brief historical transformation of the oneness doctrine. The importance of this doctrine in Confucianism should by now be a matter of no doubt. On the

52

one hand, it is the key to many seemingly unrelated problems in Confucianism, and, on the other, it can link them together under one theme. In other words, we could find in it not only solutions to many Confucian problems, but also a systematic organization in many apparently fragmentary ideas. These are the kind of methodological considerations we have in mind in our present analysis. Let us now probe this doctrine in more detail.

Dong Zhong-shu (179-104 B.C.) of the Han dynasty is the most well-known advocate of the superstitious oneness doctrine in his yin-yang Confucianism. According to him, man is the universe in miniature. The universe is regarded as an organic whole, and there is a detailed, mutually-related correspondence between Heaven or Nature and man. Regarding this correspondence, Dong said:

> Heaven completes the human body with the number of days in a full year. Consequently the body's 366 lesser joints correspond to the number of days in a year, and the twelve larger joints correspond to the number of months. Internally the body has the five viscera[14] which correspond to the number of the Five Agents. Externally there are the four limbs, which correspond to the four seasons. The alternating of opening and closing of the eyes corresponds to day and night. The alternating of strength and weakness corresponds to winter and summer. And the alternating of sorrow and joy corresponds to *yin* and *yang*.[15]

Here we can see how exact and detailed is the correspondence between Heaven and man. Man's four limbs are said to correspond to the four seasons. His twelve larger joints of the body are supposed to correspond to the twelve months. And his 366 lesser joints of the body are said to correspond to 366 days of a year, presumably a leap year. This is the most bizarre version of Confucianism ever developed in China. He also said, "When the sky is dark and it is about to rain, people want to sleep, because the material force of *yin* is at work." This is sheer nonsense. Nevertheless the oneness doctrine is truly Confucian in origin, even though Dong might have carried it too far. To show the methodological function of this doctrine, we shall illustrate how two central problems in Confucianism can be conveniently dealt with by it. One of the problems concerns the 'rectification of names' and the other is the problem of human nature.

First of all, we shall deal with the problem concerning the 'rectification of names'. For Confucius, the idea of an anthropomorphic Heaven who presides over man was always in his mind. There are numerous passages in the *Analects* referring to an anthropomorphic Heaven. For instance, on the occasion of the death of his most favorite disciple, Yan Yuan, he said, "Alas, Heaven is destroying me! Heaven is destroying me!"[16] Again, he said, "I do not complain against Heaven. I do not blame man . . . ."[17] The one passage which tends to draw a parallel between Heaven and man is this:

> Confucius said, "I do not wish to say anything." Zi Gong (子贡) said, "If you do not say anything, what can we little disciples ever learn to pass on to others?" Confucius said, "Does Heaven (*Tian*/Nature) say anything? The four seasons run their course and all things are produced. Does Heaven say anything?"[18]

The passage implies that the way Heaven operates can be emulated by man. This budding idea of the unity between Heaven and man was later developed into a full-fledged philosophical concept.

The 'rectification of names', according to Hu Shi, was the central problem of Confucius. To expound the doctrine, let us quote this other passage from Confucius:

> Zi Lu said, "The ruler of Wei is waiting for you to serve in his administration. What will be your first measure?" Confucius said, "It will certainly concern the rectification of names." Zi Lu said, "Is that so? You are wide off the mark. Why should there be such a rectification?" Confucius said, "Yu! How uncultivated you are! With regard to what he does not know, the superior man should maintain an attitude of reserve. If names are not rectified, then language will not be in accord with truth. If language is not in accord with truth, then things cannot be accomplished. If things cannot be accomplished, then ceremonies and music do not flourish, then punishment will not be just. If punishments are not just, then the people will not know how to move hand or foot. There-

fore the superior man will give only names that can be described in speech and say only what can be carried out in practice. With regard to his speech, the superior man does not take it lightly. This is all."[19]

It has been generally believed that during Confucius' time the feudal system was on the verge of crumbling. Powerful feudal princes often usurped the power of the royal family. For instance, a powerful feudal prince Ji (季氏) of Confucius' home state Lu used eight rows of dancers to entertain himself instead of six rows. According to the rules of propriety of that time, only an emperor could use eight rows of dancers for entertainment. When Confucius heard about this, he commented, "If this is tolerable, then what is intolerable?"[20] The same feudal prince was also presumptuous enough to offer sacrifice to the Tai mountain, a sacred mountain for Chinese, which only an emperor could properly do. And there were also numerous cases of regicide and patricide. All these, in Confucius' eyes, were extreme cases of social and political disorder. Therefore, Confucius took upon himself the mission of remedying the social and political disorder. He believed that the social and political disorder was the result of intellectual disorder.[21] For as the rules of conduct no longer proceeded from the central authority of the emperor, society suffered from a lack of intellectual standard. As a result, people did not know how to use the language correctly or how to perform ceremonies and music properly. Or as Confucius said in the above-quoted passage, "the people will not know how to move hand or foot." This shows the importance of restoring the intellectual order. And the way to restore this intellectual order for Confucius was the 'rectification of names'. This shows why for Hu Shi the 'rectification of names' was the central problem of Confucius.

In the process of Confucius' rectifying names, the one question which may be asked is: What are the actualities to which the names are supposed to correspond? Traditionally, the problem has never been handled in a satisfactory way. Almost anyone who is familiar with Confucius' *Analects* will be able to quote this statement, "Let the ruler be a ruler, the minister be a minister, the father be a father, and the son be a son."[22] That is, a ruler must behave like a ruler, a minister like a minister, and so on. But then how do we know how a ruler and others should behave? The orthodox Confucian answer is that the ruler should treat his subjects with benevolence, the minister should treat his ruler with loyalty, the father should be kind and gentle towards his son, and the son should be filial towards his father. If we ask further, "What are the bases for these behavioural norms?", the Zhou rules of propriety (周礼) would be referred to. Now these Zhou rules of propriety were not brought about by the Zhou people. They were the cumulative results of thousands of years of ancient Chinese culture. This is why Confucius said that he followed the Zhou system.

Hu Shi seemed to be the first one who actually related the doctrine of the 'rectification of names' to the *Book of Changes*. Concerning the relation, he gave the following two passages:

> When Pao Xi (Fu Xi) ruled over the Empire, he observed the phenomena of the heavens above and the forms on earth below; he noted the manner of birds and beasts and the products of the soil; and, receiving suggestions both inwardly from his own self and externally from distant objects, he first invented the eight *Kwas* (卦) or trigrams in order to penetrate into the mysteries of nature and to describe the reality of all things.[23]

also,

> In the *Book of Change*, the 'ideas' are symbolized in trigrammatic and hexagrammatic figures or *Kwas*, which, as we have noted, were probably the word-signs of a now extinct language. The modern equivalent of the *Kwas* is the name or word. The names are regarded as of supreme importance and their rectification is deemed a necessary preliminary to social and political reforms, because they are the symbols *par excellence* of the ideas, because in them alone are the ideas still traceable and recoverable. And to rectify the names thus means to make the names mean what they ought to mean in the light of the source-ideas which they embody.[24]

Hu Shi's view is quite clear. The legendary emperor Fu Xi, as a result of observing the natural phenomena of Heaven and Earth and the manner of birds and beasts, put down his 'ideas' in the symbols of eight trigrams. These 'ideas', according to the *Book of Changes,* are able to 'penetrate into the mysteries of nature and to describe the reality of all things'. Just as trigrams as ancient word-signs were the vehicles for carrying these important ideas, so were 'names', the Confucian equivalent for language. The only difference is that Fu Xi got his 'ideas' through observing the phenomena of nature, whereas Confucius received them indirectly through the various contributors to the *Book of Changes* including Fu Xi, King Wen, and the Duke of Zhou. The influence of the *Book of Changes* on Confucius was shown through Confucius' repeated references to that work in the *Analects.* It is therefore important to restore 'names' to its original meaning of 'ideas' as contained in the *Book of Changes,* for these 'ideas' are some sort of 'short-hand' wisdom obtained from nature by our wise ancestors.

Although the Zhou rules of propriety could also be the source for these ideas, philosophically the *Book of Changes* was far more important. For the former had already been crystallized into the customs and conventions of a particular historical period, whereas the flexibility of the meanings in the latter always allows for new interpretations suitable to different historical periods and situations. But on the whole there is no incompatibility between the two. This can be shown through the fact that King Wen and the Duke of Zhou, two rulers of Zhou dynasty, were also said to be contributors to the *Book of Changes.* We should by now understand the philosophical basis for the 'rectification of names'. Names are the vehicles for these 'ideas', which according to Hu Shi are responsible for the creation of our culture. Regarding this he has the following to say:

> The history of civilization, according to Confucius, has been a long series of successive attempts to realize the 'ideas' or perfect heavenly ideals into human instruments, customs, and institutions.[25]

This shows that civilization from Confucius' view is not just something conventional. It does have a secret channel to the principles hidden but operating in nature. For instance, the hexagram *ji ji* (既济) (after completion)☲☵, which symbolizes

57

the idea of 'success', was suggested by the overcoming of fire (*li* (离) trigram) ☲ , by water (*kan* (坎) trigram) ☵ . If we reverse the order of the two component trigrams, we have the hexagram *wei ji* (未济) (before completion)☴☶, which symbolizes 'failure'. And the institution of a marketplace was supposed to be derived from the idea of friction represented by the *li* trigram ☲(fire; hence lightning) and the *zhen* (震) trigram ☳(thunder). The invention of canoes and oars was supposed to be suggested by the idea of floating illustrated by the *xun* (巽) trigram☴(wind or wood) over the *kan* trigram ☵(water). As an illustration of how 'ideas' as short-hand wisdom of our wise ancestors are condensed in *kwas,* let us quote part of the text of this particular hexagram *ji ji* ☲☵:

> When water in a kettle hangs over fire, the two elements stand in relation and thus generate energy (cf. the production of steam). But the resulting tension demands caution. If the water boils over, the fire is extinguished and its energy is lost. If the heat is too great, the water evaporates into the air. These elements here brought into relation and thus generating energy are by nature hostile to each other. Only the most extreme caution can prevent damage. In life too there are junctures when all forces are in balance and work in harmony, so that everything seems to be in the best of order. In such times only the sage recognizes the moments that bode danger and knows how to banish them by means of timely precaution.[26]

We owe it to Dr Hu Shi for providing this philosophical foundation to Confucius' 'rectification of names'. Our concern here is rather methodological in nature, viz. how the solution of the problem hinges upon the oneness doctrine which is the Confucianists' key and organizing principle to many problems and theories. It is due to this non-superstitious or metaphysical oneness that human utensils, customs, and institutions could be derived from natural phenomena or the operations of Heaven. This illustrates our thesis that, in studying Chinese philosophy in general and Confucianism in particular, the primary task lies in searching for concepts which will cut through and link various problems and theories of different historical periods. These concepts are the organizing principles to link or systematize many philosophical problems.

The oneness doctrine can also be used to tackle the Confucian problem of human nature. Confucius said, "By nature men are alike. Through practice they have become far apart."[27] This is the first Confucian explication of the problem. Mencius stated that when we see a child about to fall into a well, we would naturally experience the feeling of commiseration or compassion. This is not because we want to find favour with the parents, nor to win the praise of our fellow villagers or friends.[28] Since we are capable of this good feeling without any ulterior motive, this was considered by Mencius a proof that human nature is originally good. The fact that many of us are unable to fully develop this good feeling does not in any way refute Mencius' thesis. It is rather the incipient moral goodness or badness that is at issue.

Had the metaphysical tendency in Mencius been fully developed, his thesis concerning the goodness of human nature would have carried more persuasive power. This task was later accomplished by the Neo-Confucianists. This Mencian metaphysical tendency is within the scope of the oneness doctrine. And it is only in the light of this doctrine that his theory can be fully appreciated. Mencius said, "He who exerts his mind to the utmost knows his nature. He who knows his nature knows Heaven. To preserve one's mind and to nourish one's nature is the way to serve Heaven. . . ."[29] This implies that there is a secret passage from our mind through our nature to Heaven. This metaphysical approach, in our view, is the one proper way to make clear Mencius' position. Unfortunately he did not elaborate in more detail upon this metaphysical tendency in his discussion of human nature.

Xun Zi gave a more systematic account of the problem than Mencius. We are not concerned with the validity of his arguments. What we like to point out is that his stress on the destructive nature of desires and passions is fundamentally empirical in nature. This empirical approach fails to take note of the oneness doctrine, which prevails in Mencius' theory of human nature. It is on this ground that he was banished from the orthodox Confucian fold. His contention that human nature is evil went against the idea of oneness between Heaven and man. This was also why the Neo-Confucianists sided with Mencius.

This controversy between Mencius and Xun Zi was not properly solved until the Neo-Confucian period of Song dynasty. The Neo-Confucian treatment of the problem of human nature resorted to the metaphysical oneness doctrine mentioned earlier, which in the view of most Confucianists solved the problem. This is another example of how this idea of oneness solved a difficult philosophical problem for the Confucianists.

In Chapter 2, I treated at some length the Neo-Confucian view of human nature. In this view, man's essential nature is the principle of life and the law of our being. It originally comes from Heaven, the ultimate source of the universe. The Neo-Confucianists solved the Confucian problem of human nature by drawing our attention to the secret channel between Heaven and man. Like the above-mentioned case of the rectification of names, the oneness doctrine once again provides the method of solution. Therefore, the right method of studying Confucianism should not be a piece-meal treatment of Confucian classics. It is of paramount importance that we deal with ideas like the oneness between Heaven and man, which can somehow link and relate the various problems, theories, and different historical versions of Confucianism under one theme. As the writings of Confucian thinkers, owing to various reasons, were never intended to be professional and systematic in nature, this is the one way we can reconstruct a system out of the outwardly fragmentary writings.

In this chapter, we have first of all traced the origin of the oneness doctrine and then briefly described its historical developments and transformations. We have next proposed the division of the doctrine into the superstitious oneness and the metaphysical oneness depending on the ascendancy of irrational or rational elements. Yet the metaphysical or philosophical subdivision handed down from Confucius, the author of the *Doctrine of the Mean*, and Mencius, to the Neo-Confucianists finally prevailed over its counterpart. In other words, the oneness doctrine as found in Neo-Confucianism represents the philosophical culmination of all the previous developments of the doctrine. The oneness doctrine is methodologically important in that it can be successfully applied to the solutions of many Confucian problems. To illustrate this point, we have shown how the application of this doctrine works in solving two important Confucian problems, i.e. the rectification of names and the issue of human nature.

Undoubtedly many other problems can be solved with the same approach. For instance, Prof. Wing-tsit Chan in his treatise, 'The Evolution of the Confucian Concept *ren'*,[30] makes great use of the doctrine 'The man of *ren* regards Heaven and Earth and all things as one body.'[31] From the implications of his analysis, the oneness doctrine can lead to the understanding of the Neo-Confucian concept of *ren,* its Buddhist influence, the issue between the Moist universal love and the Neo-Confucian *ren,* and even the difference between the Confucian 'unity with the universe' and the Taoist 'unity with the universe'.[32]

Furthermore, this oneness doctrine can also unveil the mystery as to why Chinese intellectuals are in general not enthusiastic about institutional religions, which tend to prescribe a personal God pressurizing from outside. At the end of Chapter 3, I referred to Prof. Qian Mu's observation that Confucianism has all the inspiring and expanding sentiments and functions of institutional religions. Obviously in making these observations, he has the metaphysical oneness doctrine of Neo-Confucianism in mind when human nature through *li* (principle) links with the metaphysical source of the universe, i.e. *Tai Ji* (the Supreme Ultimate). There should be no doubt that the idea of oneness between Heaven and man, which has long since left a permanent imprint upon the Chinese mind, is the most important methodological doctrine to understand Confucianism.

5

Confucian Moral Values and
Their Philosophical Justification

In order to understand the meaning of 'moral value', we should start by examining the meaning of 'value'. The use of the term 'value' is notoriously loose, ambiguous and inconsistent both in and out of philosophy. It would be a futile exercise for us to be involved and entangled in the various conflicting theories of value. For our purpose here, 'value' and 'moral value' can be defined briefly as follows.[1]

A valuable thing or idea is able to satisfy the 'inner call' of man, to evoke his responsive feelings, and finally to help him attain a pervasive and comprehensive happiness. Why is a thing of value capable of drawing out man's responsive feelings and assisting him to achieve more lasting and pervasive happiness? Human desires are various, methods of satisfying them different, and consequently the types of resultant happiness diverse. The satisfaction of one kind of desire is often not in harmony with that of another. In fact, the two may even be in conflict: they thus do not lead to what we consider pervasive happiness.

It is common knowledge that the pleasures derived from sensual indulgence are short-lived, sporadic, and frequently incongruous with one another. Thus sensual pleasures cannot result in pervasive happiness. But the sort of happiness derived from the pursuit of knowledge and aesthetic qualities is consonant with other kinds of happiness, for it enhances man's dignity and enriches his meaning of life. Therefore the pursuit of knowledge and aesthetic qualities is of value because it fosters pervasive happiness.

Although the pursuit of knowledge and aesthetic qualities is of value, it is not of moral value. Moral values are, from start to finish, social in nature: they are for the purpose of harmonizing human relationships. If a person could break away from human society and live by himself, he would not need moral values. It is part of man's nature to associate with others. This is why man could not do away with moral values. Unlike what some people may want to believe, moral values are not just the monopolized cherished qualities of moralists and conservatives.

We are sometimes under the misconception that to practise morality is for the benefit of others and not for ourselves. It is something we have to do as a result of social pressure or for fear of social sanction. From this view, to be moral is rather 'disadvantageous' to the agent. But great men of the past have convincingly shown us that to act in accordance with moral convictions is not merely in the interest of others, but primarily for our own good.

A religious believer would understand this more deeply. For instance, the ancient Greek philosopher Socrates believed that the practice of morality is in the main to pave the way for a much happier and more blissful afterlife. In his view, man's utmost concern in life must be the proper care of his soul in order to be well prepared for the journey yonder. Under this consideration, morality is of supreme importance to the agent himself.

Even for the non-religious, moral values are none the less important. Deep in human nature there is a secret yearning in man to get along well with his fellow human beings. If this longing is not properly satisfied, he will inevitably feel a sense of deficiency in life even though other desires may be fulfilled.

We have so far discussed moral values in general and their importance to man. Our next focus will be upon Confucian moral values and their justification. Among them are the familiar Confucian virtues and practice of ancestor worship and filial piety.

Ancestor Worship

For the Chinese in Singapore the memory of one's ancestors plays a rather important role in the shaping of one's life. They are often obsessed with the aspiration to glorify their ancestors with worldly success and its resultant fame. In fact many Chinese Singaporeans actually believe that the spirits of their ancestors are with them in the process of their struggles in the world. We have to know more about Chinese ancestor worship if we want to penetrate more deeply the Chinese mind here in Singapore.

In Chinese culture there have been primarily two ways of practising ancestor worship: the one practised by Confucian intellectuals and the other by the common people. Confucius' attitude towards ancestor worship is clearly shown in this passage: "Confucius worshipped the dead as if he actually felt the presence of the departed ones. He worshipped the spiritual powers as if he actually felt the presence of the powers."[2] For him, it did not really matter whether spiritual beings existed or not; what was important was the presence of a proper feeling of respect towards the object of sacrifice. This view set the tone for later Confucianists in their practice of ancestor worship.

Although Confucian intellectuals are generally indifferent to supernatural beings, they regard sacrificial rites favourably as the expression of sincerity, devotion, remembrance and love. These rites are symbolic ways of making sure that the links between us and our ancestors are not terminated by death, and that we shall continue to express our gratitude to them as the origins of our lives. This is the more intellectual approach to ancestor worship as adopted by Confucius.

The common people's belief in ancestor worship is somewhat different: they retain many of the superstitious elements of the ancient religion. They genuinely believe in the presence of their ancestors as spirits or souls during sacrifices. They are convinced that their ancestors are actually promoting their interests and assisting them in their own pursuit of worldly goals. For them a sacrifice to one's ancestors is an occasion not only of love, memory and piety, but also of asking for favours and giving thanks for blessings bestowed. The ancestral altar in many Chinese households literally means the continued presence of ancestors' spirits or souls in the on-going struggles of the living.

Although Confucianists in the elite of Chinese society do not share this superstitious belief of the masses, they are aware of its effective hold upon the latter. They know well that, without this belief, important moral values such as filial piety, kinship loyalty and family unit would suffer from a decline of their hold upon the people. Out of this consideration, Confucianists are willing to condone a belief they do not share. On the other hand, most Confucianists have some belief in Heaven and Fate (or Destiny); so the two levels of ancestor worship do have their meeting ground.

The one common consequence of Chinese ancestor worship is that, as a result of this practice, the extended family as a basic unit of Chinese society has survived for more than two thousand years. But in recent years many aspects of traditional Chinese culture have been under constant challenge and attack from Western influences. It is possible that, in the generation to come, the superstitious approach to ancestor worship will gradually lose ground and eventually die out. If ancestor worship is to survive at all, it has to drop its superstitious tint and develop its emotional, moral, social and philosophical values.

The following philosophical considerations may help transform ancestor worship into a humanistic piety towards mankind as a whole. A man's life is limited; he has no hope of living beyond a certain period of time. If he could conceptually broaden his life to include his descendants' lives, he would prolong its identity. Yet even this would not indefinitely carry forward the identity of his life. But if he is capable of the philosophical empathy to treat the entire human race as an extension of himself, he may spiritually live as long as man survives. There is hope of ancestor worship in this broadened and ultimate form being continued, generation after generation.

Filial Piety

The Confucian moral value of filial piety, the first step to practising Confucian virtues like compassion or benevolence, is for Chinese closely related to ancestor worship. It is the one virtue that has drawn much attention from the political leaders here in Singapore. It has even been proposed to incorporate the practice of filial piety into law and to take it into consideration in assigning the priority in the allocation of HDB (Housing and Development Board) flats. It is therefore clear that, from the viewpoint of the ruling elite here, this moral value is of paramount importance to Singapore.

The first question to be considered is: Can filial piety be legislated? Just as wisdom cannot be purchased, so morality cannot be legislated. Basically the spirit of filial piety cannot be legislated. Filial piety does not mean that once you stay with your parents and profitably use them as babysitters (now you can have the additional benefit of getting your HDB flat much sooner), you are then a filial son or daughter. It is the attitude of respect and genuine concern that counts. Every person because of his particular situation has his own way of fulfilling filial piety. How to discharge the duty properly and effectively is a matter of common sense and intelligence rather than morality.

But by encouraging people of three generations within the family to stay together, the government is not necessarily maintaining that filial piety can be legislated. There are circumstances under which people of two or three generations would prefer to live together but do not have the ways and means of doing so. In these cases, if the government allows them to get their HDB flats much sooner, it helps them practise filial piety and other familial virtues.

The second question to be examined is: What is the nature of Confucian filial piety? In every major culture of the world, there is a moral demand for love and respect for one's parents. But why does filial piety play such a uniquely prominent role in Chinese culture? What is the uniqueness of Chinese or, more precisely, Confucian filial piety? Is it still relevant to us today? The answers to these questions touch the core of Chinese culture.

The peculiarity of Confucian filial piety can be illustrated by the following story in the *Confucian Analects*. One feudal prince proudly told Confucius: "In my country there is an upright man. When his father stole a sheep, he bore witness against him." Confucius said: "The upright men in my community are different from this. The father conceals the misconduct of the son and the son the misconduct of the father. Uprightness is to be found in this."[3] This story seems to substantiate the belief that Confucius condoned nepotism. We would like here to argue the point from another angle. Filial piety is the root of all virtues in Confucianism. If a man does not have a sense of gratitude and affection towards his own parents, he can not be expected to harbour love and concern for others. Confucius believed that the primary moral duty of filial piety must be upheld even at the expense of other secondary moral obligations such as social justice. It is a matter of relative priority of moral values. Furthermore, filial piety is not just a moral concern within the family; it affects the moral climate of the whole society.

For the Master the importance of filial piety lies more in its spirit than its form. For instance, he said: "Filial piety nowadays means to be able to support one's parents. But we support even dogs and horses. If there is no feeling of reverence, wherein lies the difference?"[4] In those of us who consider filial piety nothing but the material support of our parents, this statement will arouse a sense of uneasiness if not shame. What Confucius wanted to stress is that filial piety ought to be a spontaneous outflow of genuine love and gratitude for our parents.

Consider another statement by the Master: "When his parents are alive, a son should not travel far away; or if he does, he should let them know where he goes."[5] Some people may think that this view is not congenial to our present society of high mobility, for it hampers the adventurous spirit of our youth today. But even now do we like our children to roam from place to place without our knowledge of their whereabouts? And, unlike the convenience and safety of modern transportation, travelling from one part of China to another during Confucius' time was usually difficult, if not hazardous. Being a seasoned traveller himself, he did not dogmatically disapprove any distant trip. He merely advised us to let our parents know where we are going, which is sensible advice even from our modern perspective.

Confucius also made the following remark on filial piety: "A son should always keep in mind the age of his parents. It is an occasion for joy (that they are enjoying long life) and also an occasion for anxiety (that another year is gone)."[6] Here he was very much a sentimentalist, not only sensitive to the nuances of human feelings but also an expert in human psychology.

After more than two thousand years, it is still relevant to ask: If a man does not even possess a sense of gratitude towards his own parents, how can we expect him to display genuine kindness and goodwill for others beyond his own family? This moral insight of Confucius is as valid now as it was to people during his time. Today, as we make great efforts to bring into being a society full of love, care and compassion in Singapore, we can learn from him the moral significance of filial piety. We are nevertheless aware that not all the minute details of Confucian filial piety ought to be followed. It is enough that we select and promote only its more pertinent and useful aspects.

A Philosophical Justification of Confucian Moral Values

Because of the announced promotion by the Government, Confucian moral values have recently attracted more attention than ever before. Unfortunately, most discussions on this subject are merely restricted to listing these moral values. Few attempts, if any, have been made to look into the philosophy behind them and justify them in these terms. The mere mention of a philosophical justification would tend to put off many laymen. But there is no reason why philosophical discussion should be off-limits to ordinary people, for with care and consideration philosophical problems can be explained in clear and simple language.

I would like here to attempt a philosophical justification of Confucian values in a way that can be easily understood. I feel this kind of justification is important, otherwise people may get the wrong impression that these values are out-of-date and have no relevance to the modern man. It is true that certain aspects of Confucianism are no longer suitable for our present society. But some of the values still hold good, and these are the ones with which I shall concern myself.

Recent studies have shown that there is a difference in ideas between Confucius and Mencius. According to this new scholarship, Confucius was a practical moralist whose primary concern was how to transform people into moral beings. He was less interested in developing a theory to justify his moral ideas philosophically.

By the time Mencius came on the historical scene, about 200 years later, other rival philosophical schools had emerged. Mencius, therefore, felt the urgency to argue against them in a more convincing manner. He considered it his mission to defend Confucian moral values with all his effort. The matter became more critical owing to the prevailing moral cynicism and scepticism. For our purpose here, I shall try to explain Mencius' theory, and use it as a pholosophical justification of Confucian moral values.

Mencius once cited the following hypothetical case to illustrate the point that all men without exception have the feeling of compassion. When anyone suddenly sees a child about to fall into a well, he is bound to have a feeling of alarm and distress, whether or not he knows the child. Most of us are not fully convinced that all men have the feeling of compassion. When

Mencius further said that a man without this feeling is not a man, we become even more sceptical. In connection with this, he did discuss three other feelings along similar lines. But in order to simplify my presentation of his argument, I shall not discuss these other feelings.

If we use clarity as the yardstick for assessing the merits or demerits of a philosophical argument, Chinese philosophers in general would not score high marks. Some modern scholars of comparative philosophy have put forward various reasons for the lack of clarity in Chinese philosophy and have even attributed the relative backwardness of science and technology in China to this characteristic.

Mencius was at least partly responsible for some of the confusion often associated with the interpretation of his philosophy. First of all, there is this mixture of descriptive and prescriptive analyses in the same context. To discuss something in the descriptive way means to describe the existing state of affairs as it is, without trying to bring in one's own value judgement. This seems to be the nature of his discussion in citing the hypothetical case of a child about to fall into the well. To discuss something in the prescriptive manner is to make a philosophical claim with the full force of one's value judgement. This is the way he argued that a man without the feeling of compassion is not a man. But when the two kinds of argument are put side by side, only through careful analysis can we avoid any confusion or misunderstanding.

I would imagine that for hundreds of years many Chinese have been confused by this sort of mixture. On the descriptive side, Mencius believed that man has moral potentials, although he did not deny that man also has other potentials like the desires and appetites for food and sex. If we simply consider the descriptive part of his argument, his view that human nature is originally good is not entirely plausible. This view can also be put in another way: man is a moral animal.

If man has all sorts of potentials, why do we only select his moral potentials as his defining characteristics? Why should we call him a 'moral animal' and not an 'eating animal' or a 'sexual animal'? After all, from what we are able to observe, man's appetites for food and sex seem to be even more powerful than his moral potentials. Hence, Mencius' descriptive argument is far from adequate in showing that man is a moral animal. But at least it has

69

made the point that, even descriptively, morality does have its basis in man's original nature.

We can only find the full force of his argument on its prescriptive side. He was simply making the philosophical claim and value judgement that only moral qualities may qualify as the defining characteristics of man. This is because moral qualities are unique in man. Mencius wanted to put up an argument that if we define man in terms of his sensual desires, there would be no way of distinguishing between man and other animals.

A Chinese would consider it imperative not to be placed in the same category as an animal like a pig. Even a Westerner, with all his animal-loving nature, may find it degrading to be so classified. Mencius' philosophical claim appears to be supported by universal human sentiments. So, why should we object to his defining man as a moral animal? In fact, we should be grateful that he had so much elevated the status of man, and given us such pride and dignity to be man.

Furthermore, both Socrates and Confucius, the pioneers of two major world cultures, seemed to cherish two ideals. First, a good man can find joy in practising moral values. Second, a good man's moral commitment is such that in certain situations he is willing to sacrifice his life for the sake of moral principles. If these two ideals are indeed true of mankind, then more people should be able to put them into practice.

If moral values are an inseparable part of man's nature, it would be much easier and more spontaneous for man to find joy in moral practice and even sacrifice his own life. This is because such joy is only the result of his natural tendencies. But if moral values are derived from socialisation and habit, it would not be as easy to experience joy in morality, let alone sacrifice his life for the sake of morality.

In the above discussion, I have merely focused upon Mencius' argument that human nature is originally good, which is the same as saying that man is a moral animal. If man is truly a moral animal, then being moral is the most natural thing for him to be. No amount of argument or persuasion would be as effective as this one point in attempting to transform members of a society into moral beings. Once this Confucian perspective has gained acceptance in the moral agent, in actual practice man would never be at a loss when deciding what are the moral things to do.

6

Moral Education in Singapore: From Religious Knowledge to Confucian Ethics

Almost out of the blue, parents in Singapore were recently awakened to the fact that religious knowledge and Confucian ethics would in future constitute an essential part of their children's moral education. Since then the one question that has been repeatedly asked is: Why? Some English-educated Chinese in Singapore have for years suffered from the deficiency of cultural and moral standards. Today as English education has become the overwhelming trend, this same problem of weakening moral ballast will grow in magnitude.

Probably in response to this undesirable state of moral rootlessness, Prime Minister Lee Kuan Yew remarked recently: "We are becoming too Westernised. We must go back to Asian virtues."[1] Some time ago he also expressed another related view: "However different the various religions, the government is in favour of a man believing in something rather than believing in nothing. I would rather have a Muslim, a devout Hindu, than a permissive atheist."[2]

These two statements clearly indicate that the government intends to promote traditional Asian values, and that it looks upon religions in general favourably. Hence, the recently announced compulsory programme of religious knowledge and Confucian ethics in secondary schools is only a logical step in this direction.

But why does the government feel dissatisfied with a secular moral education alone? An inkling of this could be detected in Dr Goh Keng Swee's reply in 1979 to Mr Ong Teng Cheong's report on moral education. The Deputy Prime Minister, Dr Goh, wrote in his reply: "To me, moral beliefs form an integrated system of thought and do not consist of a conglomeration of bits and pieces. In other words, there must be an intellectual basis which will bind the various moral qualities we deem desirable into a consistent system of thought."[3]

71

This observation has obviously set the tone for the proposed programme of religious knowledge and Confucian ethics. For a secular moral education designed even by the most competent specialists would be no match for traditional religions and cultures, which have, after all, passed the test of time.

Religions and cultures have more solid intellectual foundations and more abundant accumulated literatures. In fact, one could spend his lifetime studying any of them and still feel that his life is too short for the task. There is also this persuasive power of time-honoured tradition behind each cultural and religious system. It is not likely that a secular moral education would carry the same power.

Suppose you go and visit a foreign country where Christian culture prevails. Would it be more beneficial to have your children study their textbooks on moral education (assuming that they are not based mainly upon the Bible)? Or would it be better for them to study the Bible itself? We could understand that some parents might object to the Bible study on religious grounds if they are not Christians. But from the viewpoint of cultural understanding, to study the Bible with no intention of conversion is not the same as going to Sunday school.

For your children to learn something about the Bible is the first step to understand Christian culture and people. It is impossible to know Western culture well without some knowledge of the Bible. To claim that the only purpose for studying the Bible is to become a Christian is to take a somewhat restricted view of one's cultural development. It is possible for a non-Christian to derive immense intellectual joy and benefit out of reading the Bible.

Likewise one can never hope to grasp the subtle meanings of Chinese culture if one does not know anything about Confucianism. The same principle could apply to Buddhism, Hinduism and Islam.

In the Singapore context, moral education should, above all, aim at promoting cultural and religious tolerance and understanding. For the harmony of our society, a Confucianist should not treat a Chinese Christian as someone 'selling his soul to foreign devils' or 'shamelessly betraying his ancestors'. And similarly a Christian should not regard a non-Christian as 'immoral' or 'eternally condemned to hell'.

What is important is that students be encouraged to break out of their own cultural and religious cocoons. But how to bring about this ideal situation is a major challenge in this proposed new programme.

The recent suggestion that religions and Confucian ethics be studied comparatively seems theoretically sound to promote tolerance and understanding among different cultural groups. But it is uncertain whether any full-scale comparative study is feasible at Secondary Three and Four levels. As this involves too wide a scope, students may only be confused. After all, even at the university level comparative study is carried out only after the student has acquired certain basic knowledge of the subjects concerned.

Alternatively, before we teach students any of the six subjects, we could introduce to them the basic teachings of other cultural and religious traditions. Thus the student could at least keep the references in mind as he proceeds in his study of the particular subject. It would perhaps be easier to implement this minimum amount of comparative study.

The dilemma here is that on the one hand we do not want the students to be too narrowly compartmentalized in their respective cultural spheres; on the other it is equally objectionable that the coverage should become too broad and diffusive, with the students' energies too thinly scattered. All these are problems to be dealt with when planning syllabuses and writing textbooks. Since this is an unprecedented experiment, we can foresee difficulties. Nevertheless we must have the determination to overcome them.

We fully agree with Dr Goh's observation that moral values to be deeply embedded in moral agents should not be imparted in bits and pieces. Moral teaching is not merely an inculcation of moral rules for the solution of moral problems, but also the imparting of a coherent system of thought to serve as a general perspective for moral endeavours. Without such a perspective, moral education would fail in its most important task of instilling in students a more permanent driving force to care for the well-being of others.

On 5 December 1981, another report[4], prepared by a nine-member committee on moral education led by Dr Eng Soo Peck, head of the Institute of Education's School of Professional Studies, points out certain problem areas. There are at least six different moral education programmes now being implemented in schools here. If sub-types are taken into consideration, the present state of moral education in Singapore is rather confusing. The report further states: "While most of the programmes underscore the common aim of teaching pupils to become 'good' citizens, not all of them seem to agree on the types of values to be used to turn out the good citizen."

This confusing state of moral education in Singapore today has prompted Dr Goh Keng Swee to make the following comment at the Schools Council meeting at which the above report was presented: "Moral education is a minefield — easy to get in, difficult to get out. We are going to have to make up our minds before long, how we are going to get out of this minefield. At the rate we are going, we shall still be at square one, maybe square two at the end of the decade."[5] On 16 January 1982, Dr Goh announced the decision of the government to make religious knowledge a compulsory subject in Secondary 3 and 4, and the formation of a common moral education syllabus from Primary 1 to Secondary 2. This is a bold step for the government to take. Is it going to be more successful than previous measures? Only time will tell. It is perhaps appropriate for us here to give a brief analysis of moral education, particularly Confucian moral education.

If Socrates had been asked about his views on moral education, he would likely have mooted this question: Can morality be taught? Whether morality can be taught depends on what we think about the nature of moral values. Are moral values universally applicable or merely relative to specific situations? If moral values have universality, there is a chance that they can be taught. But if they are relative to particular situations, we can at best cultivate in students a moral insight to help them solve their individual moral problems with intelligence.

Moral education has been going on for ages whether we like it or not. In fact, the way we teach our children tends to presuppose that morality is universal. We do not instruct our children to practise a certain moral value only in certain situations. Perhaps there are parents who believe in ethical relativism and actually teach their children that moral values are valid only for specific situations, but we have yet to come across such parents. Since we have never encountered consistent moral relativists who always refrain from passing moral judgements on other people's behaviour, we shall here assume that there are universal moral values; that moral education is possible.

Chinese moral education can be taught in two ways, by the verbal method and through the moral example of teachers themselves. Teaching by moral example is generally considered the most effective. Hardly anyone objects to it. But teaching by words, the verbal method, is fraught with problems. There are two approaches to this, direct and indirect. In the 'indirect approach', students are induced to think deeply and critically about the problems and meaning of life, and to appreciate its spiritual and intellectual values, which might help check the overly materialistic aspects of our commercial life here in Singapore.

A person who is constantly examining and searching for meaning in life would usually not deviate too far from morality. That is why religion has been considered a good foundation for morality. Mr Lee Kuan Yew has shown his preference for a religious believer to a permissive atheist. Dr Goh Keng Swee also regards highly the function of religion in transforming men into moral beings. Yet one does not have to be religious to reflect upon life penetratingly. Philosophy, literature, art and other subjects in humanities are alternative ways of probing profoundly the basic problems in life.

The more direct approach of teaching by words is to implant what the teachers consider to be correct moral values in the minds of students. Traditional moral education used this approach, but such dull moralization was often rejected or at most merely tolerated. Our educationists here are aware of this defect, and have suggested story-telling to make the approach more interesting. This direct moral inculcation in various forms will continue to be used, much as it has been greatly misunderstood and abused. Many people are opposed to moral education simply because they are against its underlying uncritical moralization. With some improvements, this aspect of moral education, which is so controversial, could be conducted not only without tears but even with some joy.

To instil moral values directly in students without much reasoning may be adequate and effective when applied to lower primary students, for at this level moral education consists mainly of habit formation and character development. But when this direct approach is applied to more advanced students, moral values should be inculcated along with a philosophical foundation or rational justification. A proper understanding of the philosophical foundation could combine the fragmentary and dispersive moral concepts into a coherent system of thought.

So far educationists in Singapore have merely concerned themselves with the selection of essential moral items for planning the curriculum and writing textbooks. But we must bear in mind that in actual practice no one has ever become moral, item by item, the way we pick up things in the supermarket. We judge a person's morality on the basis of his stable moral character from which moral acts naturally flow. We do not describe a person as moral in 10 items, and another as virtuous in 10 other items. The deciding factor is whether a person subscribes to a moral point of view or whether he has cultivated in himself the care and concern for the interest and well-being of others. Even if moral values could be instilled in the minds of students in bits and pieces, they would not be prized and guarded jealously as parts of their inner beliefs. As soon as there are conflicts and temptations, without a theoretical support these values would be quickly abandoned.

Let us use more specific examples to illustrate the importance of a philosophical foundation in transmitting moral values. Many moral values promoted in our moral education here are Confucian in origin. If our teachers are not aware of the philosophical foundation behind these values, they will be groping in the dark — they might see individual trees but not the forest. But understanding this foundation they would be able to explain to students that in Confucianism there is a fine and crucial distinction between man and other animals. And for a Confucianist a man's sense of morality is what makes him a man in the true sense of the word, and what draws him apart from other animals. The students' sense of pride would motivate them to acquire the sense of morality.

As the students' intellectual understanding grows further, they should be introduced to a more sophisticated Confucian grounding. They should be led to see that according to orthodox Confucianism man is born with intrinsic moral qualities. So whether one is actually moral or not depends on the extent of his developing these intrinsic qualities. This is why for the Confucianist there is a universal claim for moral values.

Teachers may even want to use Mencius' famous example that anyone who suddenly sees a child about to fall into a well would experience a spontaneous feelings of compassion. Although Mencius regarded this as sound empirical evidence that man is universally endowed with potential moral qualities, the argument is not entirely convincing. Man has also manifested his sensual qualities that have not led Mencius to come to the conclusion that man is a sensual animal. It was actually Mencius' value judgement that man is a moral animal and thus possesses inborn moral qualities. If man does not display them in his daily conduct, he is no different from other animals. Any student who has acquired and accepted this Confucian perspective would be expected to proceed along the moral path and individual Confucian virtues would be gradually manifested in his behaviour.

The most important Confucian moral value is *ren*. This value is so central that all other Confucian moral values stem from it. To Confucius, "a man of *ren* wishing to establish his own character also establishes the character of others, and wishing to be prominent himself also helps others to be prominent."[6] This moral principle is equivalent to the Christian Golden Rule: "Do for others what you want them to do for you: this is the meaning of the Law of Moses and of the teachings of the prophets."[7]

No doubt this Golden Rule shared by both Confucianism and Christianity is universally cherished by other cultural and religious groups. While not spelling out exactly what to do, it contains a built-in criterion of reciprocity. Its validity is derived partly from the fact that the giving and receiving ends of moral interactions could be reversed without any contradiction. For instance, if an agent should commit a moral wrong he would like to be forgiven. To meet the criterion of reciprocity, the principle dictates that the same agent ought to forgive the wrong doings of others. Although on the surface this universal moral principle is empty in content, it can help one decide how to act towards his fellow men. No rational man could object to it without contradicting himself.

Since moral education has been going on for ages, we can assume the universality of essential moral values and the feasibility of moral education. Teaching by example, the more effective method, should continue to be used. The indirect approach of 'teaching by words', which encourages students to ponder over the true meaning of life, has not been sufficiently recognized as effective. In the direct approach, which has been criticized as boring moralization and therefore treated with much suspicion and impatience, moral values should, as far as possible, be inculcated with their philosophical foundation in order to achieve more effective results. In the long run, only moral values supported by rational justification and philosophical foundation will have the enduring qualities which serve as permanent rudders to guide our young through the uncertain and treacherous sea of life.

7

Confucian Ethics:
Its Core Teachings and the
New Method of Transmitting It

The Core Teachings of Confucian Ethics

What are the core teachings of Confucian ethics? Many of us are probably familiar with Dale Carnegie's best seller, *How to Win Friends and Influence People*. It discusses some of the fundamental 'techniques' for winning friends. One of the maxims is: "Always make the other person feel important." He observes that the technique, if followed, will bring us countless friends and constant happiness. And the opposite will get us into endless trouble.

Another technique is: "Show respect for the other man's opinions; never tell a man he is wrong". He promises that this rule, once obeyed invariably works wonders. He gives us many concrete examples of businessmen, who, after taking his advice, immediately boosted their sales and made a success out of their careers.

I have no doubt about the effectiveness of simple rules like these; I actually enjoy reading his books. But from the Confucian viewpoint, this is sheer prudence and not morality. To a Confucianist, moral values are intrinsically good. Practising morality ought to be for its own sake and not for other utilitarian considerations. A Confucian gentleman ought to be 'watchful over himself even when he is alone'.[1] This would not make sense if the moral agent is only concerned about the practical outcome of his action.

The above contrast could very well serve as our point of reference in outlining the core teachings of Confucius. But this is still not enough in showing us how to distinguish between Confucian and non-Confucian features in Chinese culture.

Most of us may associate Confucian ethics with filial piety, ancestor worship and the general stress upon family and human relationships. Or perhaps we are able to go one step further and

79

refer to specific moral items like conscientiousness, benevolence, love, rules of propriety, righteousness, integrity, and sense of shame. But sometimes we would attribute behavioural patterns to Confucianism that are not necessarily subscribed to by Confucius; or at most they belong to the periphery of his teachings. More specifically, we tend to be over-influenced by the many rules of propriety in our understanding and assessment of Confucianism.

Although the Master had a high regard for the rules of propriety, he was actually more concerned about their spirit than form. In the *Confucian Analects,* he would sometimes change the prescribed forms of propriety in order to adapt to the situations at hand. For instance, according to the rules of propriety, when the Confucian gentleman is mourning for his parents, it is for three days that no water or other liquid enters his mouth, and only with the aid of his walking stick is he able to rise. No one nowadays would follow this rule in its exact form. But even now most Chinese would refrain from party-going or other pleasure-seeking activities during their mourning period. Hence we still emulate the spirit of Confucian propriety.

The *Analects* is the most reliable source on the original teachings of the Master. Any attempt to understand the thought and philosophy of Confucius must begin with its study. But it is not enough to study this work alone. In order to grasp a more complete picture of Confucian ethics, we should at least study as a whole the *Four Books* as compiled by Zhu Xi (1130-1200 A.D.), the Song Neo-Confucianist. The *Four Books* comprises the *Analects,* the *Book of Mencius,* and *Great Learning,* and the *Doctrine of the Mean.* From 1313-1905 A.D., the *Four Books* had been the basis of the civil service examination in China. Practically all Chinese intellectuals during the period had to be well versed in them. To study the *Four Books* is not only for understanding the gist of orthodox Confucianism, but also to understand the Chinese mind.

The *Great Learning* and the *Doctrine of the Mean* outline Confucian orthodoxy. According to the 'three items' (三纲领) of the *Great Learning,* Confucian moral cultivation is a matter of working from one's inner self and extending to relationships with others. The first item is 'manifesting the clear character of man'. This clear character of man consists of the original moral qualities derived from Heaven. For it is stated in the *Doctrine of the Mean:* "Human nature is what Heaven imparts to man." Later Mencius specifically asserted that human nature is originally good and every man has the moral potential to become a sage. If human nature is really what Heaven gives to man, it goes without saying that this nature must be intrinsically good. This is the Confucian orthodoxy.

After one's clear character has been successfully manifested, it is only natural that he would 'love the people (or transform the people)', the second item of the *Great Learning.* As love is fully extended, there is the complete fulfillment of morality, which means 'abiding in the highest good', the third item. Therefore there is this gradual extension of moral values from the self to others. To morally transform oneself is eventually to transform others. This is particularly the case when the man is a government official or even a ruler.

The Confucian core teaching could also be put in another way. The key concept is *ren,* which has been discussed earlier. For Confucius, to practise *ren* one must, first of all, be honest with one's inborn moral qualities by developing them as fully as possible. Secondly, one must be able to extend them to others through love and considerateness. This is actually the same as the above-mentioned orthodoxy.

Mencius explained *ren* even more vividly: "All men have the mind which cannot bear to see the suffering of others."[2] This mind is what he called the feeling of compassion. Some people are able to develop and manifest this feeling whereas others are unable to do so. Here lies the difference between a Confucian gentleman and a morally inferior person. This same feeling could also apply to the running of a government by a Confucian ruler; the result would be a humane government that could not bear to see the suffering of the people.

To Mencius, a man without displaying his feeling of compassion is not a man in the true sense of the word, because he fails to develop what is characteristically human. This is the most striking difference between the Confucian view of morality and our modern belief that the formation of moral values results from socialization. Owing to this intrinsic moral inclination, Mencius argued that morality can please our minds as beef, mutton and pork can please our mouths. Consequently, a good man is able to find joy in morality.

To sum up, *ren* is the central doctrine in Confucian ethics. In Chinese medicine, physical numbness is described as 'suffering from the absence of *ren*'. In Confucian ethics, it is man's inborn moral sensitivity. Only when one has this sensitivity can one show compassion for others. In the Song dynasty, one Confucianist, Zhou Dun-yi, was so much infused with *ren* that he would not cut the grass outside his window, let alone go hunting. To another Confucianist, Zhang Zai, there was no limit to his extension of *ren* when he said: "Heaven is my father and Earth is my mother. ... All people are my brothers and sisters, and things are my companions."[3] In this regard, we recall what the Master said: "All within the four seas (the whole world) are brothers."[4] In fact, a Confucian sage would always have this feeling of compassion and harmony with the entire universe. Whatever he does carries certain cosmic significance.

The New Method of Teaching Confucian Ethics

When it comes to the teaching of Confucian ethics in moral education, it would probably take a 'systems engineer in Confucianism', metaphorically speaking, to make it work. The inculcation of moral values is one of the least understood processes in the world. Many teachers still believe that in moral education they can actually "lead a horse to water and also make him drink." But in this case the proverb is once more right: "You can lead a horse to water but you can't make him drink."

Perhaps educationists nowadays know more about how to make a person intellectual than how to make him moral. After all, we seem to see more intellectual than moral people around. As a matter of fact, most of the parents and even educationists are still groping in the dark as far as moral education is concerned. There is always a temptation for the parent and teacher to moralize, trying to implant moral values directly in children. But there is a limit to the effectiveness of this method. Some of the traditional teachers of Confucian ethics are most un-Confucian in their method: they are even more rigid than Confucius in dealing with students. We sometimes wonder if in the past Confucian values were somehow passed on to students in spite of the wrong method and not because of it.

But for our present purpose of instilling Confucian values in Secondary Three and Four students, we definitely need a new approach. We cannot expect them to learn the moral principles by heart and then follow them enthusiastically. They are far more sophisticated than that. Moralization should be sparingly applied if at all. Any value that deserves to be transmitted must pass the test of open inquiry. In other words, the student has the right to ask for rational arguments to justify the value. The teacher cannot just ram it down the student's throat. In our eagerness to transform the student into a moral being, we must as far as possible guard against any unwitting encouragement of obscurantism.

We must remember that, however important the infusion of moral qualities is, another vital function of modern education is to train students to think critically and independently for themselves. It would be unwise for us to catch one bird while scaring off another. We must try to kill two birds with one stone. And it is the method of open and rational inquiry that could promote both moral values and critical thinking at the same time.

To serve this end, it might be a good idea at the end of each lesson to set questions for open and free discussion. The discussion should be open-ended and free from presupposed values, at least during its entire length. It is up to the teacher to use his rational arguments and persuasive power to win over the student to the desirable values. Once the student is convinced of moral values through this method, the effect would last for a much longer period of time. Moreover he would also learn to think critically and independently on his own.

Another point to be borne in mind is that we should not focus upon the ephemeral details of Confucian moral practice like the rules of propriety. We have mentioned that even Confucius himself emphasized the spirit rather than the form of the rules of propriety. What is to be understood in teaching is the Confucian moral perspective and its intellectual foundation. We should allow this moral theme of 'the mind that cannot bear to see the suffering of others' to be developed and enlarged upon in our own ways.

To put the matter more concretely, it is just like shooting at a target — a moral target in this regard. What is crucial is to aim at the target and hit it right. As long as the target is accurately hit, it does not matter how one goes about reaching it. But some moral doctrinarians still insist that not only must the target be hit, but hit with a prescribed and time-honoured posture. In other words, the teacher should not be concerned too much about moral items and trivial details. For instance, it is important to show the student that in practising filial piety the spirit rather than the form should be emphasized.

It is the attitude of respect and genuine concern that counts. As one Confucianist put it, "The principle is one, whereas its manifestations are many (理一分殊)." Every person owing to his particular situation has his own way of practising filial piety. How to fulfill the moral duty properly and effectively is a matter of common sense and intelligence rather than morality. Even moral adults in general do not unanimously agree upon what is the best way of implementing it. How could we impose detailed ways of practice upon the student? It is always a good pedagogical principle to show certain respect to him and leave something to his imagination and individual decision. Otherwise the moment he sees different practices in society he will only be confused and even cynical.

Moral values such as *ren* are considered as themes to be further elaborated upon or paradigms to be aspired after in various ways rather than rules to be mechanically obeyed in a fixed manner. If moral values are considered flexible enough to be applied differently, they become the standards of moral inspiration for a moral agent without suppressing his individuality and creative thinking. Like the maxim of the Courtesy Campaign, 'Put on a smile', it is effective as it is, without going into detail as to how to smile or on what occasions to smile. An individual always knows best how to apply this maxim to particular situations if he is willing to follow it.

The other day I happened to see on my friend's office door this Confucian motto, "Do not do unto others what you do not want others do unto you." To him this is adequate as a moral theme to give him guidance without going into the specifics as to how to implement it. Yet many people are so much used to rules without knowing that following the rule is not the only way or even the best method of moral cultivation. This is particularly important to remember in teaching Confucian ethics, which were formulated in the remote past when circumstances were so much different from ours today.

8

The Relevance of Confucian Moral Values to Singapore

According to the *Census of Population 1980 Report,* out of the total population of 2,413,945 people in Singapore, there are 1,856,237 Chinese Singaporeans. This means that ethnic Chinese constitute about 77% of the total population. Another interesting outcome of this census is that no single religion is professed by more than half of the Chinese. In fact, the Chinese are the least religious when compared with the Indians and Malays. Furthermore, owing to the relative lack of religious ballast, the Chinese tend to be more easily influenced by the values and customs of other cultures.

Since 77% of the entire population here are Chinese, there is strong ground to treat Confucian moral values as the most influential values in Singapore. And the fact that the Chinese are more susceptible to other cultural influences suggests that, with the predominant trend towards English education, the Chinese relative to other ethnic groups are actually moving away from their traditional cultural values at a much faster pace. The above two reasons argue for the importance of Confucian values in Singapore.

The Singapore Government's present concern for traditional cultural values can be traced back to the circumstances leading up to the formation of the People's Action Party (PAP). The PAP was formally inaugurated on 21 November 1954 at the Victoria Memorial Hall. Before this historical event, the PAP had been under gestation for two years. Its founding members, including Goh Keng Swee, Toh Chin Chye, S. Rajaratnam, K. M. Byrne, Samad Ismail, and Lee Kuan Yew, met regularly to discuss how to organize a party with a broad appeal to all sectors of Singapore. In Mr Lee Kuan Yew's own words, their primary concern then was: "How did a group of English-educated nationalists — graduates of British universities — with no experience of either the hurly ourly of politics or the conspiracies of revolution, move people whose many languages they did not speak, and whose problems and hardships they shared only intellectually?"[1] This concern was not only political, but also cultural in nature. From the very beginning, the old guard of the PAP understood and appreciated the significance of cultural values; they were sincerely wondering how to bridge the cultural gaps between themselves and the people.

But at that time other issues of higher priority occupied their minds. They had to deal with the British, the Communists, and the communalists. Afterwards, they had to direct their principal efforts to economic developments. It was only recently, after Singapore had more or less cleared the obstacles to economic survival, that the PAP leaders began to pay more attention to the problem of cultural values. This attention has now been translated into concrete governmental actions like the intensified implementation of moral education in schools, the promotion of the Speak Mandarin Campaign and bilingualism, and the encouragement and support of cultural activities.

In a recent speech, Mr Lee Kuan Yew expressed the government's intention to grant special priority in the allocation of HDB flats to those who have their parents live with them. In explicating the reasons for this proposed new policy, he remarked: "We are becoming too westernised. We must go back to Asian virtues."[2] Mr S. Rajaratnam, the Second Deputy Prime Minister, has also on many occasions castigated Singaporeans' obsession with the pursuit of money and material ends. On one such occasion, he said: "If the average Singaporean has a philosophy at all, it has its basis in the pursuit of material wealth. Money is the source of his dreams and, I suspect, of his nightmares as well."[3] He openly professed that many Singaporeans are barbarians in the way they use money. More recently, he concentrated his criticism on the 'happy pig philosophy' of many Singaporeans who consider sensual pleasures and animal needs as the end in life. Here he made a philosophical analysis of human happiness as contrasted with the happiness of a pig:

Human happiness is of a different order altogether. It has to do with things like mind, spirit, courage, discipline, creativity, justice, law, order, achievement and civilisation. It has to do with responsibility to society — returning to society as much as, if not more than, it gave you. In fact, those who got more should give more, and those who give more than they get are the greatest of them all.

Happiness is not something which descends like manna from heaven but the fruit of effort, struggle, sacrifice, painful toil and relentless curiosity about everything.[4]

Mr Rajaratnam has previously proposed two kinds of morality — individual morality and social morality. In his view, individual morality, which is often inspired by religion, is for perfecting the individual, whereas social morality, which means accepting and obeying laws, is for promoting the well-being of the whole society. He held that social morality is more important than individual morality nowadays. It is true that part of the goal of religion is to perfect the individual, but no major religion of the world would advocate merely the individual's own perfection. In fact, most religions would proclaim that a man cannot be perfect if all his efforts are simply directed to the improvement of himself. However, Mr. Rajaratnam did not mean to take issue with religion. He was only eager to bolster up the moral value of promoting the public good in order to counter the rising tide of individualism and materialism.

To be fair to Singaporeans, they are not by nature more materialistic than people in Hong Kong or Taiwan, the other two newly industrialized and predominantly Chinese societies. It should be borne in mind that the first generation immigrants came to Singapore for the very purpose of making a living. Money-making was then understandably their major concern. Subsequently, the government's all-out efforts to promote economic growth and modernization might have unwittingly reinforced the motive to make money. Actually, it has often resorted to money as an incentive to good performance. So the dilemma and conflict of values here is how to strive for economic growth without in the meantime fostering in Singaporeans an overly materialistic outlook of life. The PAP's answer is to re-establish traditional values as cultural ballasts to keep a tight rein on the undesirable effects of economic affluence.

The government is determined to selectively preserve or revamp the traditional values and cultural experiences of the different ethnic groups here in Singapore in the light of the Western method of inquiry. This is clearly indicated by the following statement of Mr Lee Kuan Yew: "Confucianist ethics, Malay traditions and the Hindu ethos must be combined with sceptical Western methods of scientific inquiry, the open discursive method in the search for truth. We have to discard obscurantist and superstitious beliefs and practices of the East, as we have to reject passing fads of the West."[5] He tends to view religions in general in a good light. As has been mentioned earlier, he is "in favour of a man believing in something rather than believing in nothing."[6]

Being mostly English-educated, the PAP leaders' awareness and understanding of the supreme importance of traditional moral values as cultural ballast is partly in response to certain undesirable consequences of the overwhelming trend of English education. As Singapore has successfully become a financial and servicing centre, the economic value of the English language is firmly established. Moreover, in the context of a multi-racial society, English naturally emerges as the most convenient and neutral language for administrative and social purposes. Consequently the majority of parents voluntarily send their children to English-stream schools. With all its merits, English education has the one possible drawback of producing students who are 'culturally uprooted and spiritually floating'.

Professor Wolfgang Franke, the one-time Visiting Professor of Chinese Studies at the University of Malaya, had this to say about English education in Singapore: "The English education, even if it lasts thirteen years, usually remains superficial. Only a small number of outstanding students in a few eminent schools are able to penetrate to the basic values of Western culture and to acquire a genuine Western humanistic education to replace the lost Chinese one."[7]

In his view, the majority of English-educated Chinese then in Singapore suffered from the lack of fixed cultural or moral standards. He further stated: "Physically and emotionally they are Chinese, but culturally they are neither Chinese nor English nor Malay. They do not know themselves what they are."[8] He might have overstated the case somewhat, for most English-educated Singaporeans still retain certain contact with their respective cultural experiences and traditional values through their dialects and their familial and social associations. But Professor Franke was probably right in the sense that it is much easier for the English-educated here to fall between the two cultural stools, and lose their own cultural identity. Yet with the recent promotion of bilingualism and moral education, this drawback should be somewhat remedied.

In view of the above consideration, a proper examination and assessment of those prominent cultural values now exerting their influence here in Singapore is at least as important as our efforts in the economic sphere. After all, the economic fruits are meant for our enjoyment and happiness. And it is our cultural and humanistic values that can guide us in how to make use of these fruits and decide for us the kind of happiness that is worth having. For the Chinese in general, cultural values are primarily moral in nature; Confucian values are what basically shape the Chinese mind.

Owing to its confined scope, our present analysis merely concentrates upon the Confucian values of Chinese experience and does not include other cultural experiences in Singapore. But we are not unaware of the roles played by the latter. We hope that this is only the beginning; and that future investigations of a similar nature could be broadened into the Malay, the Indian and other cultural values, which also have impact upon Singaporeans. Nevertheless, it is possible that what we have drawn from the Chinese experience is universal and general enough to be harmonious with other non-Chinese experiences. If this is the case, then our study will be relevant to Singaporeans as a whole: it would be consonant with the ongoing efforts of Singapore to evolve and formulate a unique cultural and national identity.

Some of my students at the National University of Singapore have frankly told me of their doubts about the present promotion of Confucian ethics. Is Confucianism not a thing of the past? How are Confucian values compatible with our emphasis upon science, technology and economic growth? I believe many other people also share this scepticism. And it is not entirely unjustifiable for them to have such scepticism. Very few people would claim that all Confucian values are relevant to our society. To some extent, the question of the relevance of Confucianism to Singapore depends very much on how we look at the matter.

Many years ago I was a student in the United States. One day I saw a huge crowd of students browsing among several piles of books stacked on the floor. They turned out to be a very popular book called *The Joy of Sex*. A Confucian would not deny that sex is a joy to man. He would agree that by nature we desire sex. But he would argue strongly that since we share this joy with other animals, it is not characteristically human. There is another kind of joy that is uniquely human and intrinsically valuable, i.e. the joy of morality.

Many of us may think that moral practice is dull and uninteresting because it restricts our freedom and demands much sacrifice from us. Confucius did not think so. Perhaps this is one of the areas we should examine carefully to throw light upon the relevance of Confucian values today. For our life today is so full of worries and anxieties, who would not want to have some more joy, of one kind or the other? And if Confucianism can actually provide us with joy, it cannot be entirely irrelevant.

This is a rather homely and down-to-earth argument you could easily agree to. In fact, in order to appreciate Confucian values, we ought not to be too intellectually-oriented. So if you merely intend to assess the relevance of Confucian values at the conceptual level, you will not go very far. Most likely you will be disappointed. Therefore we must relate Confucianism directly to life to see its wisdom.

In the *Analects,* Confucius constantly refers to the joy of morality. To him, it is a joy, for instance, to have friends come from a distant place. He further says that the wise find joy in water; the benevolent find joy in mountains.[9] Why do the wise find joy in water? This is because water symbolizes constant changes and the wise are good at responding to the constant changes of events. Why do the benevolent find joy in mountains? This is because mountains are stable and reliable, and thus symbolize moral integrity. This characteristic is rather in harmony with the nature of the benevolent. A Confucian gentleman is free from worries and fears because he always has a clear conscience.[10] Confucius described himself as someone who was so full of joy that he forgot his worries and did not even notice the coming of old age.[11]

I have read some books by Dr Norman Vincent Peale, who is a well-known preacher and inspirational writer. He is rather persuasive in showing that Christianity can be a useful science to all modern men burdened by worries and anxieties. From our daily experience we all know that, if we can share our problems with someone we can trust, our worries can be much reduced. Now if this trusted friend is God with infinite power, our worries should be reduced even more. And Christian God, according to Dr Peale, is just such a trusted friend. It is stated in the Bible, "Come to me, all who labour and are heavy laden, and I will give you rest."[12] Another well known passage from the Psalms, "Even though I walk through the valley of the shadow of death, I fear no evil; for thou art with me."[13]

From the psychological viewpoint, a case could be made that a person with the Christian faith would have peace of mind. This is what Dr Peale considers 'applied Christianity', which in his view is relevant to all modern men. Likewise, Confucianism with all its moral tones could be made applicable to us today. With all his practical frustrations, Confucius' life was full of joy because he believed in destiny, i.e. a person should try his utmost and leave the result to destiny. Moreover, he was joyful all the time because he was convinced that whatever he did was in accordance with moral principles.

Granted that Confucianism, like Christianity, could bring us joy and peace of mind, we may still want to ask: Since Confucianism is not the only way of getting joy and peace of mind, why do we particularly promote Confucian values? First of all, we must bear in mind that Confucian ethics is only one of the six proposed options of moral education. There is no implication that as a value system Confucian ethics is superior to the other five options. Confucian ethics is a viable alternative particularly to those who have not belonged to any of the four major religions in Singapore, i.e. Buddhism, Islam, Christianity, and Hinduism. It is not meant to replace any of the four.

Secondly, we must also understand that this current promotion of Confucianism does not aim at introducing 'new values' to Singaporeans. Confucian values both relevant and not so relevant are already exerting their influences upon Singaporeans. Public discussions of these values would allow us opportunities to examine their relevance to us more carefully. If after these examinations we feel that certain values are not so relevant to us, we may still have the chance of discarding them. If current discussions of Confucian values are seen in this light, those who take exception to these values could only welcome the opportunities to voice their views and let them be known to the public and the authorities.

One Confucian value already adopted by many Singaporeans is family cohesiveness. To a Confucianist, the family unit is important because it is the training ground for morality. And filial piety is important because it is the root of morality. Theoretically, the Confucianist after fulfilling his love to his family should extend it to the country as a whole and even the world at large. But in actual practice many Chinese who would otherwise follow Confucian principles in general restrict their love only to members of the family and possibly friends. It is possible that in actual practice too much emphasis upon family has watered down a person's devotion to his society and country as a whole.

I know of one Westerner who, having lived in a Chinese society for some time, observed that the Chinese by and large are rich with human touch but short on social concern (有人情味，但是 没有公德心). In his view, the Chinese are not as public-spirited and law-abiding as their Western counterparts. To further illustrate the point, I was told that, in the old days in Shanghai before the Communist take-over, when burglars broke into a house, it would be easier to get neighbours' response by crying "Fire! Fire! Help!" rather than "Burglars! Burglars! Help!" For if one called "burglars!", the neighbours would just lock their doors even more tightly. But if it was a genuine case of fire, the neighbours would show their concern more quickly by running out to help extinguish the fire.

This shows that, in spite of their theoretical soundness, some Confucian values do not necessarily bear desirable fruit in actual practice. It is a debatable point whether Confucianism is in any way responsible for Chinese nepotism and the relative lack of social morality. But it is important that we point this out in order to guard against some possible pitfalls in the practice of Confucian values.

I would also like to use another example to show one positive impact of Confucianism. Recently it was reported in *The Asian Wall Street Journal* (12 July) that Japan's 1980 robbery rate of 1.9 per 100,000 inhabitants contrasts strikingly with rates of 243.5 in the U.S., 65.8 in France and 39.3 in West Germany. Those who have not lived in a city such as New York or Chicago before may not fully appreciate the significance of the above statistics. If Singapore's crime rate were anywhere near that of New York or Chicago, it would mean that our daughters and sisters could not safely go out at night. In fact, it would mean that even some of our male adults here would not feel safe to go to certain parts of Singapore. I hope Singaporeans would never see the day when this should happen to their city. In order to make sure that this would never happen, we should pay attention not only to the economic but also the moral climate of our society. And the moral climate of society depends entirely upon the moral character of individual citizens. Good moral character does not just come out of the blue. This is where moral education comes in and where Confucianism has a positive role to play.

That Japanese cities like Tokyo are relatively safe is partly due to the good moral character of the Japanese people, which Confucian values have helped mould, and also because of Japan's economic prosperity. In this connection, both Confucius and Mencius understood that it is not easy to morally educate a hungry man. A person must be able to feed and clothe his family before he can be led to appreciate moral values. This truth is applicable both to Confucius' time and ours. When his disciple, Zi Gong, asked about government, Confucius said, "Give them enough food, give them enough arms, and the common people will have trust in you."[14] Let us now consider the following dialogue:

> When Confucius went to the State of Wei, Ran You (冉有) (his student) drove for him. The Master said, "What a flourishing population!"
> Ran You said, "When the population is flourishing, what further benefit can one add?"
> "Make the people rich."
> "When the people have become rich, what further benefit can one add?"
> "Give them moral education."[15]

It must be noted that to have a flourishing population was considered desirable then. Here the Master also stressed the above-mentioned point that prosperity ought to be the prelude to moral education. This idea is rather relevant to our present context in Singapore.

Mencius also expressed a similar view: "Only a Confucian gentleman can be ever ready to practise morality even though he does not have constant means of material support. The common people, on the other hand, will not be so enthusiastic about morality if they have difficulty making a living."[16] From the above discussion, it is clear that, in Confucianism, material wealth and moral principles are not incompatible as long as moral principles have not been violated. Furthermore, a government would not be confident enough to launch a campaign to promote Confucian values if it has not successfully fed its people or if its leaders cannot serve as moral examples.

Confucianism is a vast and vague subject. It means different things to many different people. We may agree in general that Confucianism stresses filial piety and human relationships, particularly those relationships within the family. But the mere familiarity with moral items does not go very far in understanding Confucianism. After all, moral virtues such as filial piety and love can also be found in other ethical systems. For instance, filial piety is one of the Ten Commandments in Christianity. The Bible teaches us to love not only our friends and neighbours, but also our enemies. Therefore we should know something about the essence of Confucianism if the problem of relevance is to be discussed more than superficially. It is imperative that we get the right Confucian perspective in assessing individual Confucian values.

What then is the essence of Confucianism? According to Mencius, the greatest exponent of Confucius' thought, human nature is originally good and every man has the moral potential to become a morally perfect man. The ultimate moral ideal is *ren*, the virtue of compassion and benevolence. To attain the ideal, a person must develop his moral potential as fully as possible. And then he should try to establish rapport with others through love and considerateness. In illustrating these intrinsic moral qualities, Mencius said, "All men have the mind which cannot bear to see the suffering of others." Some people are able to develop and display this mind whereas others are unable to do so. Here lies the difference between a Confucian gentleman and a morally inferior person. To Mencius, an immoral person is not a man in the true sense of the word because he fails to develop what is characteristically human. To an orthodox Confucianist, moral values do not come from society: they are part of the original make-up of man. Moral values are therefore universal.

This belief is important in combating moral scepticism. Moral scepticism is greatly responsible for the recent trend of moral permissiveness in the West. And this scepticism is derived from scientism, the belief that scientific methods must be applied to all human spheres, including the realm of moral values. Thus when scientific methods are applied to the study of different cultures, the moral values of different cultures are considered 'relative'. If moral values are really relative, why should any person commit himself to any system of moral values? This consideration has given rise to doubts about the validity of moral values.

In our present efforts to promote moral education in Singapore, this moral relativism and thus scepticism is the principal stumbling block. The success or failure of our moral education hinges upon our teachers' ability to remove moral relativism and scepticism from the minds of our students. The major religions practised here in Singapore are all for universal moral values. This is why they are given important roles to play in our implementation of moral education. For those who do not accept any institutional religion, they may find Confucianism useful in providing arguments for universal moral values.

For a Confucianist, the cultivation of moral character is primarily for the sake of the moral agent and not for others. Science cannot answer the question: Why should one be moral? In fact, it cannot give us reasons why man should have meaning in life. But this does not prevent us from searching for the meaning in life. In the sphere of morality, science does not have the final say, and the nature of moral values cannot be determined by empirical studies.

In our present discussions of the relevance of Confucianism, some people tend to look for specific rules or precepts that might be relevant. Sometimes they even go as far as demanding that if Confucianism is relevant to them it should be able to provide specific solutions to many of their moral problems and dilemmas.

Moral dilemmas are moral dilemmas. They are not subject to easy solutions. And Confucianism is no panacea; it is not a cure-all for all our moral problems. After all, Confucius lived in an age entirely different from ours. He could not possibly have foreseen

95

all our problems with their unique features. Therefore, I would suggest that, in our consideration of the relevance of Confucianism, we should base our evaluations upon its general perspectives and themes and not its specific rules or norms, which tend to vary with historical environments. The central Confucian perspective is the importance of morality in all human activities.

We will next apply the general Confucian perspectives to the discussion of three vitally important issues in Singapore: money-making, political leadership, and 'ideal educated Singaporeans'. First of all, let us examine the value of money-making. In any thriving commercial society nowadays, money-making is bound to become one of the dominant goals in life. But does the active pursuit of this goal, often at the expense of other priorities in life, necessarily lead to the enrichment of human life itself and the promotion of comprehensive happiness that would not be in the way of the pursuit and attainment of other kinds of happiness? We have already touched upon this at the beginning of Chapter 5 when we tried to give a brief definition of moral values. How to assess and determine the nature of money-making is both important and relevant to the present situation in Singapore.

Money-making

Singaporeans have often been criticized for their presumed obsession with money-making. It was pointed out that this obsession has numbed them to the finer things in life. Yet we have also been warned with equal emphasis that money-making should not be given a dirty name, for otherwise our destiny would be like that of some third world countries where human existence is nasty and indecent.

In fact, the annual ritual of the NWC (National Wages Council) wage increment is precisely meant to give more money to the workers and wage earners. Not only are our workers concerned about this, also equally concerned are our university dons and other professionals. This has proved to be an effective incentive to higher productivity and generally been acclaimed as a means of helping establish a more equitable society. Besides, professionals in the public sector with more marketable qualifications have been encouraged to stay on with higher salaries. And the Japanese companies are much praised for giving to their workers a wide range of fringe benefits as a way of retaining the latter's loyalty. All these measures and policies presuppose that workers and wage earners could be sufficiently motivated by higher pay and more generous fringe benefits to put in harder work and better performance.

In a flourishing business community like Singapore, it is also taken for granted that businessmen's primary purpose is to make as much profit as possible. Therefore, money-making, at least on the surface, should not only be acceptable but also desirable. If so, why has it become such a convenient whipping boy in the eyes of social critics? Is money-making moral or immoral? It is about time that we ponder over its nature and implications more deeply. In one context, it is taken for granted and even openly encouraged, whereas in another it is treated as the root of many evils. What is the relationship between money-making and moral values?

The Christian Bible advises us not to store up riches here on earth, because they will not last and could be easily destroyed by moths and rust.[17] Elsewhere Jesus also said in a stronger term: "It is much harder for a rich person to enter the Kingdom of God than for a camel to go through the eye of a needle."[18] If Christians interpret these two statements literally, they may have reason to treat money-making, at least the excessive concern for money-making, unfavourably.

The Chinese sage, Confucius, stated: "Wealth and honour are what every man desires. But if they have been obtained in violation of moral principles, they must not be kept."[19] In a similar tone, he remarked elsewhere: "Wealth and honour obtained through immoral means are but floating clouds to me."[20] The Confucian attitude on money-making seems to be that, as long as wealth is accumulated without contravening moral principles, there is nothing wrong with it.

In the present setting of Singapore, the moral quality of money-making has yet to be more clearly defined. This is highly necessary and important otherwise the uninitiated may be first confused and then sceptical about the usefulness of either money-making or morality. Since at present money-making commands such strong sentiments and passions, the resultant scepticism is more likely to be directed to morality than to money-making. Anyway, either alternative is not desirable to our society.

It is as clear as daylight that business is for the pursuit of profits. If money-making is immoral, then business activities may all appear to be morally questionable. Nevertheless, it is now almost a truism that except for its manpower Singapore does not have any natural resources. Its survival depends principally on commercial activities. The more thriving they are, the more prosperous it will become. Hence, business should be in the interest of Singapore; money-making, the immediate motivation and goal of business, can only be beneficial to Singapore as a whole. Why then are all these insinuating criticisms about money-making?

The answer is that money-making is good for the country only if it complies with the law and certain moral principles. As the sanctions against illegal economic practices are well-known and explicit, we here merely touch upon the ethical aspect of business. In our ordinary human relations, we act in accordance with our moral rules and norms, which may be called 'common morality'. Likewise, business activities, at least in their ideal setting, should also be governed by moral considerations. Yet for many people 'business morality' often appears to be a contradiction in terms, because there is so much cut-throat competition and forced bankruptcy in our free market system, which does not seem to be in harmony with any morality as commonly understood by us. One conclusion seems to be that if there is any morality in business at all it cannot be the same as our common morality.

But if commercial activities under the free market system are to function in a most satisfactory manner, certain ethical principles must be attended to, the most striking and important of which is the free flow of information. For instance, the manufacturer is obliged to supply the consumers with as much relevant information about his products as possible. This is the way for him to build up goodwill among the consuming public. Actually, the company's future depends very much upon this goodwill and trust. So there are built-in moral rules even in economic activities, which may also overlap part of the contents of common morality.

One controversial result of economic activities is environmental pollution. To judge by our common morality, polluting the environment and thereby causing harm to the public health is anything but moral. But, with cost-saving and high profit as business aims, it is often understandable that a businessman would not be too concerned with environmental cleanliness, particularly when his competitors are not equally concerned. Here common morality and business morality do not seem to be compatible with each other. Sometimes, in the interest of the country, environmental purity can only be given secondary consideration, if promoting economic growth and creating job opportunities is at the time a top priority. But once the economy of a nation has advanced to the stage at which poverty is no longer the main problem, a higher priority should be allocated to the maintenance of environmental purity. In other words, the more advanced a nation's economy is, the smaller should be the gap between common morality and business morality. Since Singapore's economy has won the admiration of many countries, the moral codes of common morality should be given more and more recognition in the process of money-making.

For the Confucianist, there is a clear line of demarcation between moral values on the one hand and money-making on the other. If necessary, one should even lay down his life in order to uphold moral principles. But whether one is rich or poor is entirely determined by his destiny; consequently, material comfort should not be his main concern in life. This Confucian downgrading of material wealth has prejudiced the Chinese against commerce and money-making. In fact, in traditional Chinese social hierarchy, merchants were at the lowest rung of the social ladder, below scholars, peasants, and artisans. But, with the present ascendancy in importance of commerce in our society, successful 'merchant princes' are calling the tune in many areas of social activities; money-making has become closely related to the daily activities of many people in the commercial context of Singapore.

This is the one area where traditional values need to be redefined and revamped before they can be brought to bear upon us today. To continue the Confucian contempt for money-making is clearly an anachronism now, which may hamper economic development and modernization. Here the new value to be cultivated should be this. For an individual to be concerned with money-making is morally acceptable, as long as he regards it as the means to the end of enhancing comprehensive happiness both for himself and others.

If ends are more important than means, it then follows that not only the moral nature of money-making needs to be looked into, but also the kind of end it leads to. All too often we are only concerned with the ways and means of obtaining what we desire without seriously examining whether what we desire is really desirable. A medical doctor only cares to cure a patient's illness without pausing to determine whether this particular patient's health is worth preserving. A lawyer merely takes pains to protect his client's interests without attempting to decide whether these interests are worth protecting. A businessman's primary aim is to increase his profits and store up his wealth with no intention of finding out whether material wealth, which cannot last forever, is worth amassing.

To sum up, while there is nothing fundamentally immoral about money-making itself, there is the consideration of how to make wise use of money one has earned. Our Second Deputy Prime Minister, Mr S. Rajaratnam, commented not long ago: "Making money to make more money is sterile materialism. But using money to develop the other more important aspects of an individual's personality is to move from materialism into civilization."[21] We must be wise enough to make money serve our humanistic ends and not the other way around.

Political Leadership

The political philosophy of Confucius is another kind of Confucian value whose relevance to Singapore also deserves to be carefully examined. This is particularly true with regard to what he thought about the political leadership. To the best of Confucian tradition, moral values and political ideals are closely related: the former serve as the foundation of the latter. Confucius proposed this political recipe for a good government: the ruler must first of all set a good moral example. He specifically offered the following advice to a feudal prince: "The moral power of the ruler is as the wind, and that of the people is as the grass. In whatever direction the wind blows, the grass is sure to bend."[22] In a similar tone, he also said: "A ruler who governs his state by virtue is like the north polar star, who remains in its place while all the other stars revolve around it."[23]

But a ruler's virtue alone is not enough to make a society good. People in all walks of life must fulfill their respective social duties. This is the political implication of another remark by the Master: "Let the ruler be a ruler, the minister be a minister, the father be a father, and the son be a son."[24] The statement does not aim at maintaining the status quo in the interest of the ruler, although he would be pleased with the social and political stability that might result from such a moral order. For even a ruler himself is not exempted from performing his moral obligation. A ruler ought to be humane to his ministers, and a minister loyal to his ruler. From the Confucian viewpoint, political leaders should have their moral qualities more fully developed than ordinary people. They should be willing to sacrifice their personal interests for the common well-being of the people; most important of all, they are, at least ideally, supposed to have the wisdom to assess things in the light of everlasting values.

It would be interesting and useful to compare and contrast the above Confucian view with Plato's theory on the same subject in Western tradition. To enlighten us on the qualities of political leadership, Plato delineated for us in the *Republic* the picture of a group of prisoners at the bottom of a cave. They were tied up such that all their life they could only see the wall in front of them. Some distance behind them, a fire was blazing away. Between the fire and the prisoners, people carrying various objects walked through a passageway. The shadows were cast on the wall, and the prisoners saw nothing but the shadows.

One prisoner freed himself and turned around. At first, he could not get used to what he saw — the real objects and fire. Then he realized that what he saw previously were mere shadows. Attracted by the light outside, he struggled his way out of the cave to see the upper world. Finally he was able to face the sun. It would have been in his interest to stay in the outside world forever, but a sense of obligation compelled him to return to the cave to instruct the prisoners. But they did not believe his words, because they were only familiar with the world of shadows. They even laughed at him for his 'strange acts'.

Plato's point is this: we ordinary people are like those prisoners seeing mere shadows all our life, and the one who manages to free himself is the philosopher. The philosopher, who has the experience of the prison and the upper world, is in a better position to judge what is good. In spite of his good intention, he is often misunderstood and made fun of. He is the only one possessing real wisdom; it is he rather than others who should rule. Hence, only when the philosopher becomes a king or the king learns to become a philosopher, can a state become ideal. It is not our intention here to play up the presumed wisdom of the philosopher. The vital moral is that only the best people should be installed as rulers.

From our above description of leadership qualities in both the Confucian and Platonic traditions, we may come to the following conclusion. First, the leader should serve as the moral example. Second, he should be selected from among the best talents of the country. The two qualities have also been highlighted by Mr Lee Kuan Yew, the Prime Minister of Singapore, in his analysis of a successful leader. For instance, in his recent speech to PAP MPs after the electoral setback in Anson, he commented: "We have scoured all sectors of Singapore for talent and integrity and will continue to do so. For only the most capable, honest and committed can keep up the standards we have achieved in clean and effective administration. This team (of young leaders) is from amongst the best of Singaporeans and we shall add to it. We cannot afford to have mediocrity in charge. The system will then sag."[25]

In Mr Lee's view, the first duty of a leader is to fulfill the trust of people in him regardless of personal consequences; he should not opt for soft options in crisis. Mr Lee has specifically spelt out six basic principles for a leader to follow:[26]

(1)   Give clear signals: don't confuse people
The idea is never to confuse supporters by needless infighting and open dissension within the leadership. The leaders should always resolve their differences in private, but never contradict each other in public. So whenever they make their points in public, people will consider them more or less representing the concerted views of the leadership.

(2)   Be consistent: don't chop and change
The policies must be consistent, but not inflexible, in order to win and keep the trust of the people. The next generation of leaders must inherit the trust and not betray it.

(3)   Stay clean: dismiss the venal
The PAP government is known for its honesty, fairness, and

efficieney, which are derived from the leaders' determination not to take advantage of their positions. Whenever any official is found to be dishonest or corrupt, he must be immediately dismissed to maintain the image and integrity of the government.

(4)   Win respect, not popularity: reject soft options

The leaders should not hesitate to implement policies which may be unpopular in the short term, but are actually in the long-term interest of the people.

(5)   Spread benefits: don't deprive the people

The PAP government believes that it is not possible to practise strict egalitarianism, and that rewards must be distributed in accordance with the quality of performance. But the workers should not be deprived of their fair share of the benefits. This is the way to win the heart and trust of the people while maintaining the incentive to work harder and to develop one's talent.

(6)   Strive to succeed: never give up

Leaders ought to make their best efforts. If as a result they still do not succeed, history will forgive them. But if their failure is due to their not doing their utmost, they will only bring disgrace upon themselves.

The above political precepts for a successful and efficient leadership may have the deceptive appearance of ordinary moral platitudes, which are generally accepted as true but not expected to lead to any earth-shaking results. Yet, in the case of the first generation PAP leaders, the difference is that they have had the resolve, the perseverance, and the fortitude to act according to these principles. Their success record over the past twenty years has proven the soundness and effectiveness of these seemingly commonplace beliefs. Like Plato's philosopher king, Mr Lee Kuan Yew is confident that he knows what is best for the people, for he and his colleagues have seen the 'upper world' as a result of their past experience. They have more than once recounted this valuable experience of the past. In the above-mentioned speech to PAP MPs, Mr Lee related it again: "Several of us here around this table have walked through the valley of the shadow of death, twice: Once with the communists from 1961 to 1963, once with the communalists from 1963-65."[27]

The present PAP leaders in Singapore are predominantly English-educated. Their political style follows basically the Anglo-American system of democracy. Yet in actual practice it not only leans towards Platonic elitism, but also towards the Confucian exemplary model of virtuous rulers. This unusual mixture of Eastern and Western cultural ideals results from their keen awareness of the moral, social and political importance of traditional cultural values in a multi-ethnic society such as Singapore.

An Ideal Educated Singaporean

The relevance of Confucian moral values may also be looked at from another angle, the formation of an 'ideal educated Singaporean'. Mr Lee Kuan Yew's recent comment that Singaporeans are too westernized and therefore must go back to Asian virtues enables us to see the point in perspective. With the predominant trend of English education and their susceptibility to the influence of other cultural values, the young Chinese in Singapore tend to drift away from Confucian moral values. The danger is that they may lose their Asian cultural identity without really absorbing the humanistic core values of Western culture. They should be westernized as far as science, technology, economics, modern management and the free spirit of inquiry are concerned. An English education can facilitate their knowledge and expertise in these areas. But it would be an irreplaceable loss for them to be cut off from most of the Confucian moral values, particularly the more universal and lasting ones. Nevertheless, it would be an anachronism to demand that they be given a full-fledged Confucian grounding.

In the past few years the government has placed great emphasis upon moral education in schools. We have argued in detail in this book that moral education should have a philosophical foundation: moral values must be inculcated as part of a coherent system of thought as rightly pointed out by our First Deputy Prime Minister, Dr Goh Keng Swee. Furthermore, moral education presupposes that certain core moral values are universal in nature: they could be equally applicable to the Chinese, Malay and Indian students. One problem faced by moral universalism is how to ascertain these basic core values.

I am confident that it is possible to identify universal moral values like the above-mentioned Golden Rule, which has already been incorporated into Christian and Confucian moral ideals. Another Confucian adage, "All within the four seas (the world) are brothers"[28] could very well become a universal moral value. If certain Confucian moral values such as those to which we have just referred can be shown to be universal in nature, they are bound to contribute towards the possible moulding of the 'ideal educated Singaporean'. An ideal educated Singaporean, as far as Chinese Singaporeans are concerned, should possess the combined qualities of an educated man as emphasized in both Western and Chinese cultures. In the Western culture, an educated man is primarily one who is able to do clear and independent thinking and to appreciate the joy of knowledge. The stress is upon intellectual goodness. In the Confucian tradition of Chinese culture, an educated man is someone with a moral character. The emphasis is on moral goodness. Ideally, an educated Singaporean should acquire both intellectual and moral goodness.

Singaporeans are in a unique position to achieve the best of both cultural worlds. But if we are not adequately on our guard, we might fall between the two cultural stools and suffer the worst of both worlds. Since enough attention has already been given to the intellectual qualities in our western type of liberal education, it is imperative that we now reassert the moral values in Chinese and other Asian cultures in order to strike a proper balance.

Intellectual qualities alone cannot help us solve many of the problems in life, which often have to do with the conflict of values. Intellectual qualities have the function of clarifying certain empirical facts surrounding values, yet in the final analysis our cherished moral convictions constitute the basis for selecting from conflicting values competing for our allegiance.

I would therefore like to contend that an ideal educated Singaporean cannot do without Asian virtues such as Confucian moral values. In traditional Chinese culture, an educated man has to emulate a Confucian gentleman, who is constantly striving for moral perfection. The orthodox Confucianists hold that all men are born with intrinsic moral qualities. Certain people are able to develop these qualities and thus become moral, while others are unable to develop them and thus become immoral. If a man is immoral, he is no different from other animals. It is therefore important that an educated man is imbued with Confucian moral qualities. Although this is the traditional Chinese view of an educated man, in a less rigid form the ideal is still very much relevant and cherished in many Chinese societies today.

For a person to be transformed into a Confucian gentleman, there are certain definite steps he should follow. First of all, he has to cultivate his moral qualities. Once he has accomplished this and become a moral person, he is then in a position to regulate his family. As the family is put in good order, he will then be ready to administer the state. After the state is well governed, there will be peace and order throughout the world or at least the Chinese kingdom. Hence, for Confucianists, an educated man's first duty is to achieve his own moral goodness, and his ultimate aim to bring about world peace.

This ideal of a Confucian gentleman, while not to be promoted in its original form, is still very much relevant to modern man. Man is not just an instrument to be used as a means to an end. He is, above all, an end in himself. If a person possesses only intellectual qualities, he is nothing but a useful tool. But if he is treated as an end in himself and a free agent with a purpose in life, he needs moral values as guidance in his decision-making. Human life is full of problematic situations regarding the choice of conflicting values. This is even more so today than during Confucius' time, because our world is far more complicated. Nowadays every educated man must have basic moral values and convictions to escort him through the rough journey of life. In the Singapore context, moral goodness is as important as, if not more so than, intellectual goodness in moulding an ideal educated Singaporean. If this is granted, the relevance of Confucian values to Singapore is great indeed.

Finally, Confucianism like other ideologies has its cream and scum. The cream has been and should be passed on from generation to generation; the scum is continuously being discarded by the historical tides. To characterize the nature of this cream, let us describe the Confucian Utopia as outlined in Chapter 9 of the *Li Ji* (礼记), 'The Evolution of Rites (礼运大同篇)'. Although the ideas expressed therein are considered to be falsely attributed to Confucius and actually smack of Taoist and Moist persuasions, they could very well represent the kind of society in which *ren*

(Confucian benevolence) completely prevails. Most Chinese intellectuals are familiar with this passage: in fact, many of them have learned it by heart. It has had enormous impact upon the Chinese mind. Dr Sun Yat-sen was among those greatly influenced by it.

According to this passage, "when the Great Way reigns, the world belongs to all the people (大道之行也, 天下为公)". In this Utopia, "men love not only their parents, (but also those of others)". This is rather relevant to our present concern where many of our elderly citizens are being abandoned by their children. Furthermore, "kindness and compassion are shown to widowers, widows, orphans, childless men, and those who are disabled by disease, so that they all are sufficiently maintained." This ideal is in harmony with the kind of compassionate society we are trying to promote in Singapore.

In the economic sphere of this Confucian Utopia, "the citizens hate not to exert themselves, so they work, but not for their own profit." This is rather in line with our efforts to increase our workers' productivity. Moreover, the perfect law and order situation in that ideal society will greatly win our admiration, when it states, "Bandits and thieves, rebels and trouble-makers do not show themselves. Hence the outer doors of houses never have to be closed. This is called the Utopia." According to this Confucian Utopia, once Confucian values are put into practice, there is no fear that a country will become a 'nation of thieves'.

To sum up this chapter: what is relevant in Confucianism to Singapore is the vision and perspective, and not any detailed social, political, or even moral programmes. Perhaps it would not be considered disrespectful to hold that we moderns, knowing how to operate computers and even travel to the moon, are by no means less intelligent than Confucius. But unfortunately our high intellectual power has sometimes blinded us to the vision of and insight into the kind of society, the kind of human relations, that would make life more meaningful. In this regard, we may learn from Confucius the wisdom of treasuring man's moral values and not losing faith in his potential power for the good.

So far much has been said about Confucian ethics and its relevance to Singapore. What we have heard, up to now, are mostly positive views on the subject. Many critical observations have not been made public. It is of utmost importance that before

Confucian ethics is taught in school all the different views are freely and openly aired in our mass media. Ideally we should have as much consensus as possible regarding the desirability of Confucian ethics in general and what values to be imparted to our students in particular.

To talk about Confucian values is merely a prelude to their practice. Although it is vital that these values must be convincingly presented and argued for, our final goal is to have them serve as the guiding principles of our conduct. To achieve this goal, we should be able to see through the intellectual facades of many scholarly writings and recognize the Confucian wisdom behind them. Moral insights are not meant for intellectual discussions but to be related directly to life.

To make the most out of Confucian wisdom, we need not follow the specific rules of propriety prevalent during Confucius' time. In fact, the Master himself also selectively abided by the rules of propriety handed down to him from his predecessors. It would be against the spirit of Confucianism to follow the minute details of Confucian moral codes. It is enough to follow the Confucian perspective and to be inspired by the Confucian moral examples. Yet we have our specific ways of practising morality, which are unique to our time. If this point is well taken, many Confucian values would not be considered rigid ancient codes of morality, not relevant to our modern society.

9

The Leftist Criticisms of Confucius

People in the non-Communist world are rather familiar with all
the eulogies and tributes given to the Chinese sage, Confucius,
over the centuries. He has been universally considered one of the
greatest thinkers in the world. To many Chinese he is almost like a
god. But at the height of the anti-Confucius campaign in 1973-
1974, he was often desecrated as the 'spokesman for the aristocratic
slave-masters'. This is based upon Mao's doctrine that in a class
society every individual lives on the strength of his class status
and all thoughts are imprinted with class marks. We are now to
analyse the arguments behind this desecration to see if Confucius
was indeed the spokesman for the aristocratic slave masters.

As early as 1935 Lu Xun (鲁迅), the leftist writer much
admired by Mao, already criticized such Confucian literature as
the *Four Books* and the *Five Classics* as 'door-knocking bricks.'[1]
They were studied diligently in the past by the prospective
Confucian power elite for the purpose of passing the civil service
examinations. Confucius himself was placed on a pedestal for
worship by the powerful and influential. Once people had gained
entrance to the club of the elite, these 'door-knocking bricks'
were soon discarded. Furthermore, Lu Xun charged, Confucius'
political philosophy merely serves the interests of the ruling class,
i.e. the powerful and influential people, and not the interests of
the ordinary people.

All the leftist condemnations of Confucius are based upon
the historical assumption that Confucius had been striving for the
restoration of the 'aristocratic slavery system' of the Western Zhou
dynasty. According to Guo Mo-ruo, another influential leftist
writer, Chinese history – in accordance with the Marxist theory
of social development – can be divided into the primitive commune
period, the slavery period, and the feudal period. Due to the lack

of archaeological evidence, it is not certain under which period the Xia dynasty should be classified. But the Shang dynasty was undoubtedly a typical slavery society. During both the Shang dynasty and the early part of the Zhou dynasty, slaves were offered at sacrifices, and hundreds of slaves were forced to serve as burial companions for the dead aristocrats. This, in Guo's view, could only occur in a slavery period.

The transition between the slavery period and the feudal period roughly fell between the end of 'Spring and Autumn Period' and the beginning of 'Warring States Period'.[2] Confucius was alive during this age of transition. It is under this historical interpretation that Confucius has been criticized in China as 'stubbornly supporting the aristocratic slavery system of the Western Zhou', and condemned to symbolize all that is 'backward', 'conservative', 'reactionary', 'anti-reform' and 'anti-revolutionary'. As Confucius' concept of *ren* (humanity)[3] is not only the centre of his philosophy but also his world view, I will examine below the leftist criticisms of this concept which had paved the way for the complete denunciation of his philosophy and the relentless vilification of his historical status during the 1973 anti-Confucius campaign in China.

When Confucius once said that his doctrine was that of an all-pervading unit,[4] some disciples did not understand its meaning. Zeng Shen, known to be the most philosophically reflective of his disciples, explained it as *zhong* (conscientiousness) and *shu* (altruism), which are subsumed under the concept of *ren* (humanity). Under the Marxist microscope, *ren* represents the ideology of the Western Zhou's aristocratic slave-master class. *Ren* and *li* (Zhou rules of propriety or rites) are the two complementary concepts in Confucius' thought. *Ren* is the guiding principle of *li* and *li* is the concrete expression of *ren*. In order to understand *ren*, we must understand *li*.

In answering Yen Yuan, his most favourite disciple, as to what *ren* is, Confucius said: "To strictly subdue one's self and let one's speech and conduct completely conform to the principles of Zhou *li* is *ren*, ..."[5] Also "look not at what is contrary to the Zhou rules of propriety; listen not to what is contrary to the Zhou rules of propriety; speak not what is contrary to the Zhou rules of propriety; make no movement which is contrary to the Zhou rules of propriety".[6] Under this Marxist analysis, *li* was the moral standard for harmonizing the internal contradictions of the slave masters, and, according to *Li Ji Qu Li* (礼记曲礼), not for applying to the slaves (礼不下庶人).

Sticking to *li* is only one approach to *ren*. Another approach to *ren* is through filial piety and fraternal love. Confucius said: "Filial piety and fraternal love are the foundation of practising *ren*."[7] According to the same Marxist analysis, filial piety and fraternal love are the two ways for the aristocratic slave masters to unite themselves both vertically and horizontally. They were meant to band together members of the slave-master families. When extended and broadened to the whole society, *zhong* (conscientiousness) and *shu* (altruism) applied to those within the ranks of the slave masters. In other words, filial piety and fraternal love are ways of practising *ren* within the family, while *zhong* and *shu* are methods of practising *ren* in society. But what is the basis for maintaining that *zhong* and *shu* could apply only to aristocratic slave-masters and not to the slaves?

Zhong is generally regarded as the 'Golden Rule' of Confucius, which goes like this: "(Now the man of perfect virtue), wishing to be established himself, seeks also to establish others; wishing to be enlarged himself, he seeks also to enlarge others."[8] *Shu* is considered the 'Silver Rule' of Confucius, which goes like this: ". . . not to do to others as you would not wish done to yourself . . . ."[9] In the original Chinese texts of these two quotations, *ren* (人 : this is a different character from the previously introduced *ren* 仁 , i.e. humanity, although their English transliterations are the same) rather than *min* (民) is used to mean 'others'. *Ren min* (人民) is now used as a phrase to mean 'people'. But *ren* and *min* can also be used separately to carry roughly similar meanings. In an article 'On Confucius' written by Zhao Ji-bin (赵纪彬), Guan Feng (关锋), and Lin Yu-shi (林聿时),[10] *ren* and *min* were supposed to carry two entirely different meanings during Confucius' time. At that time, according to them, *ren* was used to refer to the aristocratic slave-masters, while *min* to the slaves. Therefore, if only *ren* appears in the above quotations, *zhong* and *shu* are meant to apply to the aristocratic slave masters and not to the slaves. And since *zhong* and *shu* are the methods of practising *ren* (humanity), the class nature of *ren* (humanity) is thereby clearly manifested.

To support this position, they point out that in the entire *Confucian Analects* 'to love *min*' (爱民), to love slaves according to their interpretation, never appears. They maintain that only one passage in the *Confucian Analects* seems to contradict this position. This passage reads like this:

> Zi Gong said, "Suppose the case of a man extensively conferring benefits on the people, and able to assist all, what would you say of him? Might he be called the man of humanity?"[11]

Here *min* (slaves), rather than *ren* (aristocratic slave masters) appears in the original Chinese text. But then Confucius replied immediately, "Why speak only of humanity in connection with him? Must he not have the qualities of a sage? Even Yao and Shun were still solicitous about this."[12] They take this to mean that in Confucius' view the idea of 'extensively conferring benefits on the people (*min*, i.e. slaves), and assisting all', (博施於民而能济众) was impracticable and out of touch with the social reality of that time. And almost in the same breath, Confucius continued, "Now the man of humanity, wishing to be established himself, seeks also to establish others; wishing to be enlarged himself, he seeks also to enlarge *others.*"[13] Here *ren* (aristocratic slave masters), rather that *min* (slaves), is employed (corresponding to the above translation 'others').

They also cite other passages from the *Confucian Analects* to illustrate this difference of usage between *ren* and *min*. For instance,

> The Master said, "The *people* may be made to follow a path of action, but they may not be made to understand it." (民可使由之，不可使知之)[14]

Also

> The Master said, "To rule a country of a thousand chariots, there must be reverent attention to business, and sincerity; economy in expenditure, and love for men; and the employment of the people at the proper seasons". (节用而爱人，使民以时)[15]

In the first quotation, *min,* meaning slaves, is used (corresponding to the above translation 'people'). So *min* might be 'made to follow a path of action', but not 'to understand it'. This is an example of the character *min* being used to refer only to the lower class people, i.e. slaves. In the second quotation, in the context of 'love for men', *ren,* which means aristocratic slave-masters, is used (corresponding to the above translation 'men'), while, in the context of 'the employment of the people', *min* is used (corresponding to the translation 'people').

Therefore, in the view of these anti-Confucius writers, for Confucius the aristocratic slave-masters were the objects of love, whereas the slaves were the objects of employment or manipulation. They then make an important qualification that should Confucius have had any love for slaves, it was merely a concessive gesture on the part of the slave masters. This seems to weaken their argument, for then the problem of how to distinguish between genuine love and mere concessive love arises.

They also cite another passage to illustrate that Confucius did not love all people:

> The Master said, "It is only the man of ren (humanity), who can love and hate people."[16]

The man of *ren* (humanity) here refers to men like Confucius. According to their interpretation, although Confucius talked about 'loving people' he did not mean to love all people. As a thinker of the slave-master class, Confucius never genuinely loved all people.

It is significant that Feng You-lan, the well-known Chinese philosopher, took issue with the above Marxist slant of Confucius.[17] His main contention is that before the Spring and Autumn Period, i.e. Confucius' time, the meanings of the two terms, *ren* (人) and *min* (民), might be different from their present usage, but since that period their meanings have not fundamentally changed. Feng holds that even today *ren* and *min* do not carry the same meanings. The meaning of *min* (民) has the connotation of political status, while that of *ren* (人) does not have this connotation. For instance, when we want to say that there are patients in the hospital, we say *bing ren* (病人) rather than *bing min* (病民).[18] Again when we say that the student body of a certain school has the total of ten thousand people, we use *yi-wan ren* (一万人 ten thousand people) rather than *yi-wan min* (一万民).

These two examples show that *ren* (人) even in the Spring and Autumn Period was used to refer to people in general rather than the 'aristocratic slave-masters'. Feng then mentions some phrases current at that period to further argue this point. For example, people living in the city were called *guo ren* (国人). People living in the countryside were addressed as *ye ren* (野人). Aristocrats were named *da ren* (大人). Slaves and peasant slaves were designated *xiao ren* (小人). So if *ren* is interpreted as 'aristocratic slave-masters', then *ye ren* would mean rural aristocratic slave-masters and *xiao ren* would mean small aristocratic slave-masters. This does not seem to be compatible with the general usage of these phrases at that time.[19]

Feng also refutes one self-contradictory point of Guan Feng and Lin Yu-shi. According to Guan and Lin, Confucius was raising the banner of *ai-ren* (爱人 : loving people) to harmonize contradictions between different classes. But if *ren* meant only 'aristocrats' at that time as they assert, then *ai-ren* would mean only 'loving aristocrats'. And if this was the case, how would Confucius' raising the banner of *ai-ren* manage to harmonize class contradictions? In other words, if Confucius wanted to harmonize class contradictions, he should have advocated loving people of different classes. But then Feng concedes that although Confucius claimed to love all people, 'people' (*ren*) here was only taken in an abstract sense. For all practical purposes, Confucius could only love exploiting classes. But this does not mean that *ren* (人) was used to refer to the 'aristocratic slave-masters' in Confucius' time.

Feng also qualifies what Guan and Lin say about the previously quoted passage, 'extensively conferring benefits on the people, and able to assist all, . . .' Feng agrees that in Confucius' view this was an impracticable position out of touch with the social reality of that time. But this was because the practice of this doctrine required the fulfilment of certain economic conditions. Confucius did not mean that we ought not try to carry out this doctrine of extensively 'benefiting and assisting the people'. And if so, Confucius' doctrine did not seem to represent the ideology of slave-masters. For the latter could only treat slaves as the instruments of production, and not human beings to be loved.

So Confucius, at least in theory, was willing to confer *ren* (humanity) upon the slaves. During the transitional period between the slavery system and the feudal system,[20] this positive attitude, in Feng's view, should be commended.

Another point at issue was regarding the passage, "It is only the man of *ren* (humanity), who can love and hate others"[21] which, in the view of Guan and Lin, means that Confucius did not love all people. Feng's interpretation of this passage is quite different: "It is only the man of *ren* (humanity), who can like good people, and who can dislike bad people." In his view, this 'like' and 'dislike' must be interpreted on the basis of the broader Confucian context of 'loving all people'. Feng also disagrees with Guan and Lin's interpretation of *ren* (人) in the Golden and Silver Rules of Confucius: "wishing to be established himself, (he) seeks also to establish others; wishing to be enlarged himself, he seeks also to enlarge others", and "not to do to others as you would not wish done to yourself". *Ren* (人) here means 'others' as clearly shown in the original Chinese text, and does not mean 'aristocratic slave-masters' as claimed by Guan and Lin.

Feng's objections to the above anti-Confucius criticisms are significant for two reasons. First, he has been widely considered the best and most original Chinese philosopher of our time. His scholarship in Chinese classics and academic competence are well recognized. Second, as he has shown to be receptive of the political situation in China after 1949, his comments on anti-Confucius criticisms cannot be lightly dismissed as 'anti-communist' bias. As a matter of fact, he did reflect in his writings some of the official lines of the anti-Confucius dogmas. For instance, he maintains that Confucius was a philosopher of the exploiting class, and therefore could not transcend the standpoint and interests of exploiting classes. Towards members of his own class, Confucius might subdue himself (and return to propriety).[22] Towards working people, he was most selfish. When he advised working people to 'subdue themselves', he actually wanted the working people to be contented with exploitation.[23] These anti-Confucius sentiments of Feng You-lan tend to offset all his previous positive comments on Confucius.

If Feng You-lan's rebuttal of the above anti-Confucius criticisms is valid, the thesis that Confucius was the spokesman for the aristocratic slave-masters cannot stand. The internal contradictions of these criticisms as pointed out by Feng effectively render the criticisms inoperative. It seems that most of the anti-Confucius writings after 1949 generally followed an official ideological guideline. In them Confucius was blamed for not serving the proletarian cause. There is no doubt that Confucius could not live up to the standards of Marxism. But those who are even slightly familiar with the *Confucian Analects* cannot by any yardstick label him the spokesman for the aristocratic slave-masters. There may be some truth in the observation that in Chinese history some Confucianists actually put themselves at the service of aristocrats and did not attend to the interests of the masses. But there is no basis whatsoever for assuming that Confucius himself set the bad example. The fact that he came from a dispossessed aristocratic family does not thereby imply that his philosophy must be in the interests of those aristocrats. We have to judge him on the basis of what he actually said and taught. To most people, his sayings and teachings tend to delineate a different picture of him.

In an article entitled "Viewing Confucius' Creative Spirits" from the *Book of Changes'* (从周易看孔子的创造精神),[24] Thomas H. Fang (方东美) revives the Neo-Confucian thesis that Confucius' best philosophical contributions are contained in his *Ten Wings*[25] In his view, the *Confucian Analects* can only represent the practical wisdom of the young Confucius, and those trying to trace Confucius' thought only in the *Confucian Analects* are complete laymen. This is like trying to trace Socrates' essence of thought in his early fragmentary sayings.[26] He called the Confucianist the 'time-man' to be distinguished from the Taoist whom he called the 'space-man'. He describes a Confucianist as follows:

> To characterize a Confucian as the 'time-man' is to keep in line with Mencius' description of Confucius as the 'sage of time'. In his commentaries on the *Book of Changes* Confucius often said: 'the meaning of time is really profound'. For, whichever age he happens to be at, a Confucian always tries to grasp its spirit. He wants to throw all the lives of the universe and human activities into the flow of time seeing how they develop, how they change, and how they create.

116

The fundamental thought of the Confucian is to express this active, creative spirit of the 'time-man'.[27]

After comparing this interpretation of Confucius and his thought and that of the leftist scholars in China, we may ask ourselves: "Are they dealing with the same Confucius or not?" One interpretation of Confucius is that he was pure, spiritual transcendental, and only interested in things like the 'active, creative spirits of life'. This can be seen in what Fang said in the same article:

> Everywhere in the *Ten Wings* Confucius was advocating active, creative spirits of life and developing a great long flow of cultural life. The historical continuity expressed therein enables the series of Twenty-Five Dynastic Histories (二十五史) to maintain an unbroken link in the flow of time. There can never be found a second case in the whole world.

With this high praise, Confucius must be regarded as a sage. Another interpretation of Confucius is that he prepresented merely the interests of the aristocratic slave-masters, and that he was the chief advocate of class exploitation. This demand for Confucius to serve the proletarian cause is politically motivated. Besides these black and white descriptions, can he be painted somewhat in grey?

There is no basis whatsoever for characterizing Confucius as the spokesman for the aristocratic slave-masters. Confucius' teachings, if not distorted for political reasons, clearly show that he was genuinely concerned about the suffering and political and social chaos of his time. His main aspiration was to restore order through moral transformation and the general 'rectification of names', so that a ruler could once more behave like a ruler, a minister like a minister, a father a father, and a son a son.

If because of this he should be accused of preserving the status quo and thereby benefiting the aristocrats, it was entirely contrary to his intentions. But this does not mean that he is immune to any criticisms. In fact, during the May-Fourth Movement in China (c 1917-1919), Confucius was severely blamed for the backwardness and many cultural defects in China. Many of the criticisms then were raised under the banner of science and democracy. It seems that these are better grounds for censuring the Master than those put forward by the leftist scholars in China. To many of these scholars during 1973-1974, the fact that Confucius came from a dispossessed aristocratic family determined his class status permanently. He was also out of favour with them for not serving the proletarian cause more earnestly.

10

A Critical Analysis of the Traditional View on Chinese Culture

We are living in an age in which material progress is considered part and parcel of the culture. Hence the cultural content taught in our schools must not be divorced from this thinking. Otherwise what the students learn will not be relevant to their future needs. More specifically, in defining Chinese culture to our students we must give due recognition to both its spiritual and material aspects so that it will become relevant today.

I have reason to believe that 'relevance' is not a respectable term among some highbrows. The moment it is mentioned, they would waste no time condemning it as polluting the 'pure, sacred' air of the 'most lofty' culture. This is particularly true in the way that Chinese culture is discussed by some Chinese intellectuals. In their private life, they enjoy the modern conveniencies that make up our present notion of good life. When they are to choose a place to settle down, they would study closely its economic and political conditions, and the relative buying power of their remuneration before they make their move. They would also find out about the laws governing migration if the prospective green pasture is a foreign country.

Their behavioural patterns are in general guided by practical and materialistic considerations, but in their intellectual moments they regard culture as 'an expression of the objective spiritual life of mankind'.[1] In discussing Chinese culture, they keep emphasizing the 'lofty religious spirit', the 'intrinsic spiritual worth', the 'internal spiritual life', and 'transcendental activities', of Chinese culture. As a result, they condemn atheism and material efficiency as culturally anti-Chinese. Furthermore, they seem to unjustifiably play down the roles of the common people in the constitution of Chinese culture. For instance, they blame the Westerners' misunderstanding of Chinese culture on their lack of opportunities 'to make close contacts with Chinese who could represent her (China's) cultural spirit'.[2]

Now let us take a close look at this view on Chinese culture. If this view were true, millions of Chinese people would at best be living on the periphery of Chinese culture, which would be paradoxical if not contradictory. It is true that intellectuals can understand and express in verbal terms Chinese culture better. But there is no ground whatsoever for holding that therefore they alone can 'represent' the Chinese cultural spirit. It is precisely this view that led some Chinese scholars to argue that Chinese culture was very much alive because they themselves were in self-consciousness very much alive.'[3] And when they were forced to take refuge abroad during the political cataclysm of the communist take-over of China in 1949,[4] they considered it one of the greatest setbacks of Chinese culture.

John Dewey, the American philosopher, once posed these two questions: What has culture to do with the daily tasks of millions of harassed pupils and teachers preoccupied with the routine of alphabetic combinations and figuring? What bond is there between culture and barren outlines of history and literature?[5] It seems that the same questions can also be asked today. 'Alphabetic combinations and figuring' are still the primary concern of most students nowadays and 'barren outlines of history and literature' the major concern of students in humanities. To those Chinese scholars mentioned above, these subject matters would apparently have little if anything to do with culture. Like the critics of Dewey's time, they would be quick to condemn the 'voluntary surrender of our educational system to utilitarian ends, its prostitution to the demands of the passing moment and the cry for the practical'.[6]

Now must we really apologize for the voluntary surrender of our educational system to utilitarian ends, to the demands of the passing moment and the cry for the practical? I personally do not think so. There is nothing dishonourable, shameful, or anti-cultural for educationalists to publicly promote economic growth and industrialization and to orient their educational programmes accordingly. It would indeed be impractical and a misplacement of priorities to stress the 'internal spiritual life' and 'transcendental activities' when a large section of society is suffering from material privations. What is at issue here is not just a matter of determining priorities between cultural and non-cultural activities, but one concerning the very scope of culture itself.

The issue is: Does culture include science and technology or does it consist merely of humanistic activities such as art, literature and philosophy? In our view the range of culture includes both categories, i.e. science and technology, on the one hand, and humanistic activities, on the other. Consequently, the choice between the two categories is not one between cultural and non-cultural activities, but one between two different kinds of 'cultural' activities. Therefore, the choice should not be considered as an either-or situation, but a situation concerning priority and balance between these two categories. The attempt to define culture in terms of 'internal spiritual life' unnecessarily narrows the scope of cultural content and activities. It simply picks out one cultural aspect and treats it as the whole, meanwhile condemning the other aspects as 'uncultural'. This cultural view has been embraced by many Chinese intellectuals who have a Confucian orientation in their ideology.

In a society like the United States, the overall wealth of the country is enormous although the distribution may still be a problem. Even in such a relatively well-to-do society, Dewey believed that there was no turning back as far as the emphasis on science and technology went. Therefore, there is not need for us in a less developed country to apologize for the emphasis on science and technology in our school curricula. As Dewey said very well:

> Science makes democracy possible because it brings relief from depending upon massed human labor, because of the substitution it makes possible of inanimate forces for human mascular energy, and because of the resources for excess production and easy distribution which it effects.[7]

It is clear from his account that, living in a society of democracy, we must incorporate science into the content of our culture and hence into our school curricula. The leaders of the 'May Fourth' movement of 1919 in China were right in promoting Mr Science and Mr Democracy, although many conservative Chinese scholars thought that as a result of the above promotions, these leaders neglected the religious element in Chinese culture and thus the internal spiritual life, which serves as a foundation for Chinese ethico-moral principles.

What these scholars are concerned about are the 'intrinsic spiritual worth', the 'spiritual life', and the 'religious element' in Chinese culture. It is significant that they seldom refer to the livelihood and the cherished values and beliefs of the general masses in their discussion of Chinese culture. It is only in passing that they would pay some lip service to science and technology. As a matter of fact, they tend to frown upon pragmatism, utilitarianism, materialism and naturalism, which are all undeniable elements of the political and social life of a modern society. This can be illustrated in the following remark by them:

> Furthermore, those leaders of the May Fourth movement were more or less inclined to admire 'science and democracy' while in their philosophical resort believed rather in pragmatism, utilitarianism, materialism and naturalism. Hence, their interpretation of Chinese culture was chiefly set in the light of lacking religious faith. Levelling against the ancient moral principles, they attempted to wipe them out as social evils which appeared in the form of decadent rituals and harmful customs. They likewise treated Chinese ethico-moral patterns as sheer formalities of external behaviour without any intrinsic, spiritual worth.[8]

Although they do not openly criticize these leaders, their remarks concerning the May Fourth movement unmistakably show their disapproval. And their argument for the existence of democratic and scientific traditions in Chinese culture is at most evasive. They simply ignore the fact that traditional Chinese culture needs to be transformed in the direction pointed out by the leaders of the May Fourth movement. Let us consider another passage by the same scholars:

> We acknowledge that historical Chinese culture lacked the modern Western democratic system, Western scientific study, and the current practical skills in technology. As a result, China has been unable to attain real modernization and industrialization. However, we still cannot acquiesce in the charge that in the Chinese ideal state the notion of democracy was lacking, or that the internal aspiration of

Chinese political development did not urge the establishing of a democratic system. Nor can we acknowledge that Chinese culture is anti-scientific, radically contemptuous of technical skills.[9]

This is the typical argument followed by those who believe that all the good things on earth like science and democracy must already be contained in Chinese culture. Although they admit that traditional Chinese culture lacks democracy, science, and technology, they nevertheless maintain that Chinese people have the aspiration and internal potential to create and develop all these good things and many others. Many of them are so complacent with this line of reasoning as not to face up to the fact that traditional Chinese culture, in spite of its many perennial qualities, badly needs a transformation in order to fit into our modern society. Dewey's criticism of traditional Western culture applies equally well to traditional Chinese culture:

> The old culture is doomed for us because it was built upon an alliance of political and spiritual powers, an equilibrium of governing and leisure classes, which no longer exists. Those who deplore the crudities and superficialities of thought and sensation which mark our day are rarely inhuman enough to wish the old regime back.[10]

He further adds:

> And while there is no guarantee that an education which uses science and employs the controlled processes of industry as a regular part of its equipment will succeed, there is every assurance that an educational practice which sets science and industry in opposition to its ideal of culture will fail.[11]

Many old fashioned intellectuals believe that culture must be set above politics and economics. This view has traditionally held sway over the cultural circle. Yet, according to Dewey, the cultural question is, first of all, political and economic in nature before it can be considered cultural.[12] We are well aware of the influence exerted by politics and economics upon our daily life. If culture is to be set above politics and economics, it is nothing but the frosting on top of the cake of economic and political substructures. In other words, it would merely be a superficial adornment to the other facets of human life.

Although this cultural view was generally accepted in the past, it should not remain so now. The emphasis on science and technology does not necessarily downgrade the spiritual aspects of culture. It does so only if a division between the spiritual and the material is presupposed. In fact, there should not be any demarcation between the two realms. The humanistic activities, which are generally considered to belong to the 'spiritual', often involve material elements, and vice versa. For instance, is a museum spiritual or material? The cultural qualities and historical meanings in the exhibits are certainly 'spiritual' if the term is interpreted in its proper sense. What about the building and the material substrata of these items? If they are taken away, can the spiritual aspects remain? Likewise is a library with all its collections spiritual or material?

Furthermore, science and technology involve more than the material aspects of factories and machines. There are intellectual activities, spiritual qualities, and even humanistic touches behind the designs of factories and machines. Hence we can see the naivety of those who believe that science and technology may desecrate the spiritual aspects of culture. The problem is whether besides science and technology we should also pay attention to other cultural activities such as art, literature, and philosophy.

Many Chinese intellectuals like those critics during Dewey's time deplore the material primacy as causing the crisis in culture. It is true that we do have a cultural crisis now. But the problem does not lie in the material primacy. The problem, according to Dewey, is: How do we make the material an active instrument in the creation of the life of ideas and art?[13] The emphasis on science and technology is already an irreversible trend. If we should subscribe ourselves to the dualism of the spiritual and material in order to satisfy our cravings for a 'more spiritual culture', we can only take 'occasional sabbatical leave' escaping to the past or to those places where this kind of culture is better maintained. Dewey described the cultural critics of his time in this way:

> Many American critics of the present scene are engaged in devising modes of escape. Some flee to Paris or Florence;

others take flight in their imagination to India, Athens, the Middle Ages or the American age of Emerson, Thoreau and Melville. Flight is solution by evasion. Return to a dualism consisting of a massive substratum of the material upon which are erected spiritually ornamented facades is flatly impossible, except upon the penalty of the spiritual disenfranchisement of those permanently condemned to toil mechanically at the machine.[14]

Many Chinese intellectuals dissatisfied with the present Chinese cultural atmosphere have other ways of escape. They flee to the perennial spiritual realm of Chinese classics. Their American counter-parts take only occasional imaginative flights, while in actual life they are still very much American, i.e. materialistic and pragmatic. Some of the Chinese intelligentsia take permanent flights to Chinese classics, the cultural realm of Being, and expect, like Plato, the changing world of Chinese society to conform to their eternal standard. I have no intention of underestimating the wisdom contained in Chinese classics. Anyone familiar with the cultural heritage in China can not but be attracted by the wisdom of Confucius, Lao-Tzu, and Chuang Tzu. But their wisdom is not perennial in the sense of having the constant powers of a cure-all. The moment Chinese culture is treated as something fixed and eternal, as something belonging only to the past, it is good only for museum exhibitions.

The perennial nature of Chinese culture lies rather in the incessant interactions between the past wisdom and the present social environment. There is no doubt that one can do excellent academic research in Confucianism, Taoism, or Buddhism on a campus in Boston, Chicago, or Berkeley. It is possible that in one's research one may turn out good theoretical results concerning culture heritage in China. But whether the results are applicable to the present Chinese scene or not is rather problematic. It would be irresponsible for a Chinese scholar in Boston to dictate to his fellow Chinese back in China, where he may not have set foot for many years, what cultural direction they should take. While Chinese scholars can continue doing whatever they are doing in Boston, Chicago, or Berkeley, and contribute in some way to Chinese culture, they should be aware of their limitations and should maintain a more modest attitude.

So far we have levelled our criticisms at two main aspects of the traditional view on Chinese culture: first, the overemphasis on the spiritual and transcendental values of culture at the expense of the roles played by science and technology; second, the overlooking of the cultural roles played by the general masses in terms of their cherished beliefs, values, and life patterns. The overemphasis on the material, like science and technology, is as detrimental to culture as that on the spiritual. Yet, Dewey, in spite of his emphasis on science and technology, explicitly warned against any educational system turning out 'industrial fodder', which would only aggravate the problem of building a modern culture.[15]

The theoretical basis of my criticism on the first point is an attempt to balance the humanistic values with science and technology in creating a new culture relevant to modern men. We all know very well that some of the cultural problems are generated by a lack of concern for humanistic values rather than by any deficiency of science and technology. But this does not in any way compromise our central theme that any culture to be relevant to modern men must incorporate these two realms of values into its make-up. It is too obvious to be denied that the present problems concerning over-population, the shortage of food and energy, and environmental pollution can not be solved without science and technology. As a matter of fact, their solution depends mainly on science and technology.

There are arguments put forward to defend the traditional view on Chinese culture. Concerning our criticism of the overemphasis on the spiritual value of culture, one argument points out the concern over the Military Industrial Complex in America as indicating the undercurrent against science and technology in Western culture. This much publicized Military Industrial Complex is mainly due to the lack of control by the civilian government over the rather selfish alliance between the Military and the profit-motivated Big Business. What the Military and the Big Business desire is a war economy which will perpetuate the stupendous power of the former and the huge profits of the latter. The problem does not directly hinge on science and technology themselves. Although some intellectuals, especially those in the field of humanities, have shown their concern over some of the undesirable results of science and technology, I fully share Dewey's view that the emphasis on them in our modern culture is an irreversible trend. Only those who are so out of touch with the present social reality that they fail to see the importance of science and technology can plead for any reversal of the present trend.

Another argument has been espoused to justify the dismissal of the participation by the general masses in the formation of a national culture. According to this argument, the intellectuals are like the doctors who have the specialized training and qualifications to analyse and interpret the cultural symptoms as displayed by the activities of the general masses who are more or less like patients. While this analogy is helpful and, if interpreted in a certain sense, can be correct, the intended result does not necessarily follow. To pursue this analogy, there are at least two kinds of doctors. One kind of doctor holds fast to the out-dated, unscientific, or pseudo-scientific medical theories handed down to him from generations ago and regards them as medical cure-alls. He does not want to bother himself with any new developments or discoveries in the medical field. Very often he does not even bother to examine closely the very patients he is supposed to treat. He prescribes the same kind of medicine that was used to treat the ancients to treat the moderns believing that what is good for the former must also be good for the latter. He tends to disregard any new developments or discoveries in the field and ignore the unique characteristics of each medical case and the changing nature of a certain disease because of spatial or temporal pecularities. He is what we call a quack doctor.

The second kind of doctor is exactly the opposite. He is the one we would like to consult with about our medical problems.

To return to the context of our main discussion, taking the cherished beliefs, values, and life patterns of the general masses into consideration in the formation of culture would not necessarily deprive the intellectuals of their 'doctor's status' concerning culture. It simply points out that the raw materials of culture must in the final analysis be related to the daily activities of the general masses no matter how crude or homely these materials are. In the process of creating a new culture, the present social conditions and environment must, as far as we can, be taken into consideration. The culture of the ancients must not be rigidly imposed upon the moderns. It is all the more objectionable if the intellectuals attempt to treat the creatures of their own imagination produced in their cloistered ivory towers as the essence of culture and expect the general masses to follow the cultural norms thus prescribed.

To sum up, although the term 'culture' can be defined in many ways and it is difficult to give it a precise and generally agreed definition, the treatment of 'culture' as 'an expression of the objective spiritual life of mankind' tends to neglect the material aspects of culture, and to overemphasize the roles played by intellectuals in 'representing' the cultural spirit. Most objectionable of all is the attempt to treat culture in such a way that the general livelihood, and the cherished values and beliefs of the general masses are completely swept aside as if they were at best living on the periphery of the culture.

In a way, Ernst Cassirer's approach to culture is more satisfactory. He regarded culture as the various forms of communal human existence, which are used to organize man's feelings, desires, and thoughts. These forms are contained in language, in myth, in religion, in art, in science, and in history. Man is defined in terms of human culture. Philosophy of man is in a way also philosophy of culture, which, according to Cassirer, "would give us insight into the fundamental structure of each of these human activities, and which at the same time would enable us to understand them as an organic whole."[16] Furthermore, Cassirer maintained that if human nature of 'essence' is to be defined, the definition can only be understood as a functional one, not a substantial one.[17] If this cultural approach is accepted, any reference to the 'intrinsic spiritual worth' or the 'internal spiritual life' of Chinese culture is irrelevant. One of the advantages of this approach is that human activities are easily open to studies and observations, while the metaphysical nature or 'spiritual worth' of man, if there is any, may lead to all sorts of controversial and inconclusive debates. Cassirer's approach also has the advantage of stripping the intellectuals of their pretensions to 'represent the cultural spirit', and giving back to the general masses their deserved role in the cultural life.

128

Footnotes

Chapter 1: What is Confucianism? (A Bird's-Eye View)

[1] Besides the present usage, the 'six arts' (*Liu Yi* 六艺) also means 'six classics', which include the *Book of Changes*, the *Book of Poetry*, the *Book of History*, the *Book of Rites*, the *Book of Music*, and the *Spring and Autumn Annals*.

[2] Wing-tsit Chan (ed.), *A Source Book in Chinese Philosophy*, Princeton University Press, Princeton, 1963, p. 108. For convenience of reference, I shall throughout the book make use of Chan's translations in the *Source Book* whenever possible. When I do so, his name will be put in parentheses as (Chan).

[3] For a detailed discussion of this concept, see Wing-tsit Chan's article, 'The Evolution of the Confucian Concept *Jen*', *Philosphy East and West*, Vol. 4, No. 1 (Jan, 1955), The University Press of Hawaii, pp. 295-319 (*Jen* is the same as *ren* in this book.)

[4] *Confucian Analects*, 1:2 (Chan, pp. 19-20).

[5] *Ibid., 1:3* (Chan, p. 20).

[6] *Ibid.*, 3:3 (Chan, p. 24).

[7] *Ibid.*, 4:3 (Chan, p. 25).

[8] *Ibid.*, 13:27 (Chan, p. 41).

[9] Cf. Shu-hsien Liu's article, 'A Philosophical Analysis of the Confucian Approach to Ethics', *Philosophy East and West*, Vol. 22, No. 4 (Oct. 1972), pp. 417-425.

[10] Wei-ming Tu, '*Li* as a Process of Humanization', *Philosophy East and West*, Vol. 22, No. 2 (April 1972), p. 195.

[11] *Analects*, 6:28 (my translation).

[12] *Ibid.*, 12:2 (my translation).

[13] *Ge-wu* is usually translated as the investigation of things. As its meaning has been controversial, here we prefer to retain its original Chinese term.

[14] *Mencius*, 2A:6 (Chan, p. 65, The word 'feeling' in the translation has been replaced by 'heart'.).

[15] *Ibid.*, 7A:1 (Chan, p. 78).

[16] (Chan, p. 523).

[17] Fung Yu-lan, *A Short History of Chinese Philosophy*, The Free Press, New York, 1966, p. 43.

[18] *Analects*, 4:15 (my translation).

[19] Cf. Chen Da-qi (陈大齐), *Collections of Studies on Confucius' Doctrines* (孔子学说论集), Zheng Zhong Book Co., Taipei, 1961, p. 55.

20 *Mencius*, 6A:11 (my translation).

21 Cf. *Mencius*, 7B:31.

22 (Chan, p. 119).

23 (Chan, p. 120).

24 (Chan, p. 121).

25 Burton Watson (Translator), *Basic Writings of Mo Tzu, Hsun Tzu, and Han Fei Tzu,* Columbia University Press, New York and London, 1967, p. 89 (*Hsun Tzu* is the same as *Xun Zi* in this book).

Chapter 2: Confucian Views on Human Nature

1 *Confucian Analects*, 17:2, in Wing-tsit Chan (ed.), *A Source Book in Chinese Philosophy*, p. 45.

2 A.C. Graham, 'The Background of the Mencian Theory of Human Nature', *Qing Hua Journal of Chinese Studies* (清华学报), New Series VI, No 1 & 2 (Combined Issue), December, 1967, The Qing Hua Journal Publication Committee, Taipei, Taiwan, p. 224.

3 Fu Si-nian, *Xing Ming Gu Xun Bian Zheng,* (性命古训辨证), The Commercial Press, First Edition, 1940, Vol. 1, (main text) p. 1-a.

4 *Ibid.*

5 *Ibid.*, p. 40-b, 37-a.

6 *Mencius*, 6A:3 (Chan, p. 52).

7 Graham, 'The Mencian Theory', p. 218.

8 Graham's translation from *Huai-nan-zi* (淮南子), ch. 13, *Ibid.*, p. 220.

9 *Ibid.*, p. 224.

10 *Mencius*, 3B:9 (Chan, p. 72).

11 *Ibid.*, 6A:3 (Chan, p. 52).

12 *Ibid.*, 6A:4 (Chan, p. 52).

13 *Ibid.*, 2A:2.

14 D.C. Lau, *Mencius,* Penguin, Middlesex, 1970, p. 238.

15 *Mencius*, 6A:2 (Chan, p. 52).

16 *Ibid.*

17 *Mencius*, 2A:6 (Chan, p. 65).

18 *Ibid.* (Chan, pp. 65-66).

19 Arguing along the same line, D.C. Lau points out: "Mencius ought, of course, to show that by nature man in fact possesses these four beginnings. Unfortunately he has done so only in the case of the heart of commiseration." 'Theories of Human Nature in Mencius and Shyuntzyy', *Bulletin of the School of*

Oriental and African Studies, University of London, Volume XV: Part 3, The School of Oriental and African Studies, London, 1953, p. 549.

20 Guo Mo-ruo, *The Book of Ten Criticisms* (十批判书), People's Publishing Agency, 1954, pp. 215-217.

21 *Ibid.*

22 The *Xun Zi,* 'The Nature of Man is Evil', (Chan, p. 129).

23 *Ibid.*

24 Graham, 'The Mencian Theory', p. 545.

25 *Ibid.,* p. 548.

26 *Ibid.*

27 *Ibid.,* p. 550.

28 *Ibid.*

29 Cheng Yi *et al., Reflections on Things at Hand* (近思录), Compiled by Chu Hsi (same as Zhu Xi) and Lu Tsu-ch'ien, Trans. with notes by Wing-tsit Chan, Columbia University Press, New York and London, 1967, p. 28.

30 'Principle' is the most important concept in Neo-Confucianism. For a detailed treatment of it, see 'The Evolution of the Neo-Confucian Concept of *Li* as Principle', in *Neo-Confucianism, Etc: Essays by Wing-tsit Chan,* Oriental Society, U.S.A., New York etc., pp. 45-87.

31 *Yuan, heng, li* and *zhen* were translated by Wing-tsit Chan as Origination, Flourishing, Advantage and Firmness respectively, and by the late J. Percy Bruce as Origin, Beauty, Utility and Potentiality.

32 Zhu Xi, *Zhu Xi Quan Shu* (朱子全书) (Complete Works of Zhu Xi), 42:2b (Chan, p. 612).

33 *Ibid.,* 42:6a (Chan, p. 614).

34 *Ibid.,* 42:6b (Chan, p. 614).

35 *Ibid.,* 42:4b (Chan, p. 613).

36 J. Percy Bruce, *Chu Hsi and His Masters,* Arthur Probsthain & Co., London, 1923, p. 210.

37 Zhu Xi, *Quan Shu,* 42:3b (Chan, p. 613).

38 *Ibid.,* 43:4a (Chan, p. 624).

39 *Ibid.,* 43:15b, 16a.

40 *Ibid.,* 43:18a (Chan, p. 626).

41 Homer H. Dubs, *Hsuntze: The Moulder of Ancient Confucianism,* Arthur Probsthain & Co., London, 1927, pp. 77-110. (Hsuntze is the same as Xun Zi in this book.)

42 Lau, 'Theories of Human Nature', p. 550.

Chapter 3: The Confucian Concept of 'Immortality' and Its Cultural Implications

1 *Analects,* 11:11. In Wing-tsit Chan (ed.), *A Source Book in Chinese Philosophy,* p. 36.

1963, p. 36. For convenience of reference, whenever I use Chan's translations in the *Source Book,* I shall put his name in parentheses.

2 *Zuo Zhuan* Xiang Kung (襄公) 24th year. The three immortalities are to be distinguished from the hereditary fief of a feudal prince (世禄), which might be handed down from one generation to another and yet is not immortal.

3 Lin Yutang (ed.), *The Wisdom of Confucius,* The Modern Library, New York, 1938, p. 105.

4 *Mencius,* 2A:2 (Chan, p. 63).

5 *Ibid.,* 6B:15 (Chan, p. 78).

6 *Ibid.,* 7A:1 (Chan, p. 78).

7 *The Xun Zi,* Ch. 17 (Chan, p. 120).

8 Carson Chang, *The Development of Neo-Confucian Thought,* Bookman Associates, New York, 1957, p. 212.

9 *Ibid.*

10 Chan, *Source Book, p. 643.*

11 *Analects,* 6:20 (Chan, pp. 643-644).

12 *Ibid.,* 11:11 (Chan, p. 644).

13 Chan, *Source Book,* p. 644.

14 Hu Shi (胡适), *Hu Shi Wen Xuan* (胡适文选 /Literary Selections of Hu Shi), Hong Kong: Xian Dai Shu Dian (现代书店 / Modern Book Store), no date listed, pp. 65-73.

15 *The Straits Times,* Singapore, February 24, 1977, pp. 7-8.

16 Lin Yutang, *The Importance of Living,* Reynal & Hitchcock, New York, 1937, p. 401.

17 Chan, *Source Book,* p. 497.

18 Qian Mu (钱穆), *Hu Shang Xian Si Lu* (湖上闲思录 /Leisurely Reflections on a Lake), San-Min Book Company/ 三民书局 , Taipei, 1969, pp. 102-103 (my translation).

19 *Ibid.,* p. 105.

Chapter 4: The Confucian Harmony and Union between 'Heaven and Man'

1 *Confucian Analects,* 17:19, in Wing-tsit Chan (ed.), *A Source Book in Chinese Philosophy,* p. 47.

[2] Fung Yu-lan (also Feng You-lan), *A Short History of Chinese Philosophy*. edited by Derk Bodde, The Free Press, New York, 1966, p. 208.

[3] *Ibid.*, p. 132.

[4] *Ibid.*, p. 133.

[5] *Xun Zi*, Ch. 17, 'On Nature' (Chan, p. 116).

[6] *Ibid.* (Chan, p. 120).

[7] Fung, *A Short History of Chinese Philosophy*, pp. 210-211.

[8] *Ibid.*, p. 210.

[9] Bertrand Russell, *The Basic Writings of Bertrand Russell*, edited by Robert E. Egner and Lester E. Denonn, Simon and Schuster, New York, 1967, p. 255.

[10] Hu Shi, 'The Scientific Spirit and Method in Chinese Philosophy', *The Chinese Mind*, edited by Charles A. Moore, East-West Center Press, University of Hawaii, 1967, pp. 104-131.

[11] *The Doctrine of the Mean* (Chan, p. 98).

[12] *Mencius*, 7A:1 (Chan, p. 78).

[13] *Mencius*, 7B:38.

[14] Heart, liver, stomach, lungs, and kidneys (Chan, p. 282, footnote).

[15] Dong Zhong-shu, *Chun Qiu Fan Lu* (春秋繁露) (*Luxuriant Gems of the Spring and Autumn Annals*), Ch. 56 (Chan, pp. 281-282).

[16] *Analects*, 11:8 (Chan, p. 36).

[17] *Ibid.*, 14:37 (Chan, p. 43).

[18] *Ibid.*, 17:19 (Chan, p. 47).

[19] *Ibid.*, 13:3 (Chan, p. 40).

[20] *Ibid.*, 3:1 (my translation).

[21] Hu Shi, *The Development of the Logical Method in Ancient China*, Paragon Book Reprint Corp., New York, 1963, p. 22.

[22] *Analects*, 21:11, p. 39.

[23] Hu Shi, *The Development of the Logical Method in Ancient China*, p. 36 (originally in the *Book of Changes*, App. 1, pt. II, 2).

[24] *Ibid.*, p. 60.

[25] *Ibid.*, p. 37.

[26] *The I Ching* or *Book of Changes*, the Richard Wilhelm Translation rendered into English by Cary F. Baynes, Routledge & Kegan Paul Ltd., London, 1951, p. 245.

[27] *Confucian Analects*, 17:2 (Chan, p. 45).

[28] *Mencius*, 2A:6.

[29] *Ibid.*, 7A:1 (Chan, p. 78).

[30] Wing-tsit Chan, *Neo-Confucianism, etc.: Essays by Wing-tsit Chan,* Compiled by Charles K.H. Chen, Oriental Society, New York, Hong Kong, etc., pp. 1-44.

[31] *Ibid.,* p. 20.

[32] *Ibid.,* p. 21.

Chapter 5: Confucian Moral Values and Their Philosophical Justification

[1] For a brief and yet clear analysis of 'moral values', refer to *The Concept of Morality* by Pratima Bowes, London: George Allen & Unwin Ltd., 1959, pp. 118-125.

[2] *Confucian Analects,* 3:12.

[3] *Ibid.,* 13:18.

[4] *Ibid.,* 2:7.

[5] *Ibid.,* 4:19.

[6] *Ibid.,* 4:21.

Chapter 6: Moral Education in Singapore: From Religious Knowledge to Confucian Ethics

[1] Mr Lee Kuan Yew's speech to the People's Action Party Members of Parliament on the by-election defeat of the Anson Constituency (published in *The Straits Times* of Singapore, 14 December 1981).

[2] *Far Eastern Economic Review,* Hong Kong, August 1-7 1980, p. 54.

[3] *Report on Moral Education 1979,* prepared by Mr Ong Teng Cheong, Minister for Communication and Chairman, Moral Education Committee, 1 June, 1979, p. iii. The quotation is from the reply to the Report by Dr Goh Keng Swee, Deputy Prime Minister and Minister of Education.

[4] *The Sunday Times,* Singapore, 6 December, 1981.

[5] *Ibid.*

[6] *Confucian Analects,* 6:28.

7 *Matthew,* 7:12.

Chapter 7: Confucian Ethics: Its Core Teachings and the New Method of Transmitting It

[1] *The Doctrine of the Mean,* Chapter 1.

² *Mencius*, 2A:6.

³ This is from the *Western Inscription* (西铭), which is originally part of ch. 17 of the *Cheng-meng* (正蒙). It was inscribed on the west window of Chang Tsai's lecture hall. For its English translation refer to *A Source Book in Chinese Philosophy* by Wing-Tsit Chan, p. 497 and also Fung Yu-Lan's *History of Chinese Philosophy*, vol. 2, pp. 493-495.

⁴ *Confucian Analects*, 12:5.

Chapter 8: The Relevance of Confucian Moral Values to Singapore

¹ *People's Action Party 1954-1979*, 25th Anniversary Issue (Singapore: the Central Executive Committee, People's Action Party, 1979), p. 31.

² Mr Lee Kuan Yew's speech to the People's Action Party MPs on the by-election defeat of the Anson Constituency (published in *The Straits Times* of Singapore, 14 December 1981).

³ *The Sunday Times*, Singapore, 28 June 1981.

⁴ *The Straits Times*, Singapore, 9 December 1981.

⁵ *Far Eastern Economic Review*, Hong Kong, August 1-7 1980, p. 54.

⁶ *Ibid*.

⁷ Alex Josey, *Lee Kuan Yew: The Struggle for Singapore*, Third Edition (London, Sydney, Melbourne, Singapore, Manila: Angus & Robertson Publishers, 1980), p. 96.

⁸ *Ibid*.

⁹ *Confucian Analects*, 6:21.

¹⁰ *Ibid*., 12:4.

¹¹ *Ibid*., 7:18.

¹² *Matthew*, 11:28.

¹³ *Psalms*, 23.

¹⁴ *Confucian Analects*, 12:7.

¹⁵ *Ibid*., 13:9.

¹⁶ *Mencius*, 1A:7.

¹⁷ *Matthew*, 6:19.

¹⁸ *Ibid*., 19:24.

¹⁹ *Confucian Analects*, 4:5.

²⁰ *Ibid*., 7:15.

²¹ *The Sunday Times*, Singapore, 28 June 1981.

²² *Confucian Analects*, 12:19.

²³ *Ibid*., 2:1.

24 *Ibid.*, 12:11.

25 *The Straits Times*, Singapore, 16 December 1981.

26 *People's Action Party 1954-1979*, p. 38.

27 *The Straits Times*, Singapore, 16 December 1981.

28 *Confucian Analects*, 12:5.

Chapter 9: The Leftist Criticisms of Confucius

1 Lu Xun, *Lu Xun San Shi Nian Dai* (鲁迅三十年代集/*The Collected Works of Lu Xun in the Thirties*), (Hong Kong: New Art Publishing Company/新艺出版社, 1968), Volume 8, Part 2, p. 103. 'Door-knocking bricks' refer to bricks used to knock on the door and thrown away when they have served their purpose – stepping-stones to success.

2 Guo Mo-ruo, *Nu Li Chi Shi Dai* (奴隶制时代/*Slavery Period*) (Peking: People's Publishing Agency/人民出版社, 1972), pp. 1-2.

3 *Ren* has been variously translated as love, virtue, perfect virtue, humanity, benevolence, or human heartedness. For simplicity's sake, we shall here use "humanity" as the uniform translation of *ren*.

4 *Analects*, 4:15.

5 *Ibid.*, 12:1.

6 *Ibid.*

7 *Ibid.*, 1:2.

8 *Ibid.*, 6:28.

9 *Ibid.*, 12:2.

10 The Editorial Staff of Zhong Hua Book Publisher (中华书局), *Kong Zi Zhe Xue Tao Lun Ji* (孔子哲学讨论集/*The Collected Works of Studies on Confucius' Philosophy*) (Peking: Chung Hua Book Publisher, 1962), pp. 217-270.

11 *Analects*, 6:28.

12 *Ibid.*

13 *Ibid.*

14 *Ibid.*, 8:9.

15 *Ibid.*, 1:5.

16 *Ibid.*, 4:3.

17 Feng You-lan's counter view was given in an article 'On Confucius' Concept of *ren* (仁); which also appears in *The Collected Works of Studies on Confucius' Philosophy*.

18 *bing* means 'sickness', whereas *ren* has the meaning of 'person' or 'people.' (In Chinese language, nouns do not show any distinction between singular and plural). Thus *bing ren* means 'patients.' Here *bing min* is hardly used to substitute *bing ren*.

[19] *Ibid.*, p. 289.

[20] According to Fan Wen-lan, the Chinese historian, the first feudal system was established in the Shang dynasty. But at that time the feudal system was secondary to the slavery system. It was during Confucius' time that the feudal system gradually began to replace the slavery system.

[21] *Analects*, 4:3.

[22] *Ibid.*, 12:1.

[23] *The Collected Works of Studies on Confucius' Philosophy*, p. 293 and 296 (my translation).

[24] This article was written by Thomas H. Fang, the late Professor of Philosophy, National Taiwan University, formerly Professor of Philosophy at National Central University in Nanking and Chunking. It appeared in *Central Daily News*, Taipei, Taiwan, in three installments, Jan. 20, 21 and 22, 1974.

[25] *Ten Wings* refers to the Commentaries of the *Book of Changes*. There has been a debate as to whether Confucius actually wrote this work or not. To date no conclusion has been found. Meanwhile, most contemporary scholars including Wing-tsit Chan, author of *A Source Book in Chinese Philosophy*, have accepted the *Analects* as the most reliable source of Confucius' teachings (Cf. p. 18 of *A Source Book in Chinese Philosophy*, Princeton University Press, 1963).

[26] Professor Thomas H. Fang's aforementioned article, Jan. 22 1974, footnote IV.

[27] *Ibid.*, Jan. 20 instalment (my translation).

Chapter 10: A Critical Analysis of the Traditional View on Chinese Culture

[1] Carson Chang, *et al.*, "A Manifesto on the Reappraisal of Chinese Culture", *Chinese Culture: A Quarterly Review*, Vol. III, No. 1, October 1960, Taipei, p. 34.

[2] *Ibid.*, p. 16.

[3] *Ibid.*, p. 9.

[4] *Ibid.*, p. 3.

[5] Reginald D. Archambault, ed., *John Dewey on Education: Selected Writings* (with an introduction by the editor) (New York: Random House, Inc., 1964), p. 289.

[6] *Ibid.*

[7] *Ibid.*, p. 293.

[8] Chang *et al.*, *op. cit.*, p. 16.

⁹ *Ibid.*, pp. 35-36.

¹⁰ Archambault, ed., *op cit.*, p. 293.

¹¹ *Ibid.*

¹² John Dewey, *Individualism Old and New* (New York: Capricorn Books, 1962), p. 124.

¹³ *Ibid.*, p. 126.

¹⁴ *Ibid.*

¹⁵ *Ibid.*, p. 127.

¹⁶ Ernst Cassirer, *An Eassy on Man* (New Haven and London: Yale University Press, 1969), p. 68.

¹⁷ *Ibid.*